# STONES OF WITNESS

## Images of the Holy Land

# STONES OF WITNESS

## Images of the Holy Land

TEXT AND PHOTOGRAPHS BY

## STEWART CUSTER

BJU PRESS
Greenville, South Carolina

**Library of Congress Cataloging-in-Publication Data**

Custer, Stewart, 1931-
   Stones of witness : images of the Holy Land /text and photographs by Stewart Custer.
      p. cm.
   ISBN 1-57924-673-7
      1. Israel--Description and travel. 2. Israel--Pictorial works. I. Title.

   DS107.5 .C87 2002
   915.69404'54--dc21

                                                    2001056500

All Scripture is quoted from the Authorized King James Version.

Photo Credits:
Dome of the Rock Interior 137 (top), Cistern at Masada 164 (top left), courtesy of Art Directors & Trip Photo Library

**Stones of Witness: Images of the Holy Land**
Stewart Custer, Ph.D.

Design: Jeff Gray and TJ Getz
Interactive CD: Jeff Gray, Jon Kopp, and Brannon McAllister

© 2002 by Bob Jones University Press
Greenville, South Carolina 29614

Printed in the United States of America
All rights reserved

ISBN 1-57924-673-7

15   14   13   12   11   10   9   8   7   6   5   4   3   2   1

TO MY DEAR WIFE,

CAROL,

INTREPID TRAVELER

WONDROUS SUITCASE ORGANIZER

BELOVED LIFE COMPANION

# CONTENTS

# PREPARATIONS FOR TRAVEL

Stones of Witness: Images of the Holy Land *is the result of my leading eight tours to the Holy Land. Each tour lasted from twenty-one to twenty-eight days. Since the average Holy Land tour is from seven to ten days, we were able to visit many more places than the average tourist gets to see. Often the tourist goes at Christmastime or during the spring, when rainy days, or dull gray days, are the rule, but we always went in the summer, when every day was a bright sunny day, perfect for taking photographs. If you are planning a trip to the Holy Land, this book will help you prepare for what to look for and what position to get to in order to take good photographs. If you have already been to the Holy Land, this book will bring back rich memories and will augment your travels with views of places that you did not get to see because of shortness of time. Since these tours were study tours, we will point out the biblical significance of the places visited, which most tours fail to mention. If you have no present hope of going to the Holy Land, this book will help you to envision the setting in which many biblical events occurred.*

*Most Holy Land tours concentrate on the "shrines," where there are lines of tour buses parked and multitudes of people waiting to get in. It is refreshing to go also to out-of-the-way places that are important to see because of their biblical background, to find only native Israelis or Palestinians there, and to see only a chance schoolbus with children on a field trip to a historical place.*

*My prayer is that the following photographs will make the Holy Land come alive for the reader. Everywhere you travel in the Holy Land there have been prophets and apostles there before you. You will have the chance to see the very places where Jesus walked. "Let the words of my mouth, and the meditation of my heart, be acceptable in thy sight, O Lord, my strength, and my redeemer" (Ps. 19:14).*

# UNDERSTANDING THE LAY OF THE LAND

In any travel it helps to know the landscape, elevation, and climate of the region. When you think of the Holy Land, think of 30° N latitude (Florida, south Texas). Beersheba in the south is on a level with Port Said in Egypt. On the other hand, the elevation of the Galilean hills is close to that of Asheville, North Carolina (cool and refreshing). In the middle of the night, you may be surprised to hear the mountain wind moaning outside your bedroom window and reach for a blanket! The same day may be very warm in the afternoon sun. In the dry climate of the Holy Land, the temperature may fluctuate thirty to forty degrees during a day. When you watch the sound and light performance in Jerusalem in the evening, remember to take a sweater with you.

If we could take a vertical slice east and west across the Holy Land, we would find that it starts at sea level at Ashdod in the coastal plain, slowly rises through the piedmont region to the central highlands at Jerusalem (2500 feet), then drops through switchbacks down the Jericho road to the level of the Dead Sea (1300 feet below sea level), and then climbs by

more switchbacks up to the Transjordanian mountains (2500+ feet), where Amman, Jordan, lies on a highland plain.

On one tour we deliberately traveled from Amman, Jordan, to the border at the Allenby Bridge, across the land over the highlands at Jerusalem, down through the piedmont region to the coastal plain in one day, to give the group the sense of the differing elevations of the land. To extend our investigation north and south, we need to examine a map carefully to see these differing aspects of the land. The coastal plain runs along the Mediterranean Sea. In the north it is interrupted by a low hill at Rosh ha Niqra at the Lebanon-Israeli border. The plain extends down to Mount Carmel, which is a spur of the highland regions that extend all the way to

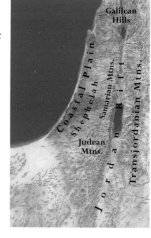

the coast, effectively dividing the plain into two parts. From Mount Carmel southward it is called the Dor plain, the Sharon plain, and the Philistine plain. Going eastward, we come to the Shephelah, the piedmont, a slowly ascending incline to the hill country. Beth Shemesh and Lachish were important cities of the Shephelah. The central highlands start from the Lebanon and Anti-Lebanon mountain ranges, Mount Hermon being the most impressive landmark, and extend southward through the Galilean hill country. The valley of

Armageddon (or Esdraelon) interrupts these highlands. Southward, the Samaritan hills continue to Jerusalem, and the Judean hills on southward to the Negev Desert.

The Jordan rift is the lowest place on the face of the earth. There are two parallel fault lines north and south, one on each side of the Dead Sea. These faults have allowed the land to be 685 feet below sea level at the Sea of Galilee, slowly deepening to about 1300 feet below sea level at the Dead Sea, the lowest point on earth. The deepest point of the Dead Sea is 1300 feet below its surface. Geologists have determined that below that level is a large amount of sediment deposited by the Jordan River, so originally the Dead Sea was much deeper than it is now. That fault line extends southward into the Red Sea at Eilat and down the Red Sea into Africa, ending near Victoria Falls 4000 miles away! It is no wonder that there are evidences of earthquakes all over the Holy Land. There are hot springs at Tiberias along the Sea of Galilee and others at the En Gedi region along the Dead Sea, which indicate continuing geological activity.

The Transjordanian highlands start in the north at Mount Hermon and extend southward on the east bank of the Jordan rift. The ancient kingdoms of Moab and Edom were on that side of the Jordan River. Toward the south the rose-red city of Petra lies in the midst of mountainous terrain.

Wherever you travel in the Holy Land, you will find rocks underfoot. Those rocks are a good indication of the geological makeup of the land. It helps to be able to identify some obvious ones. The photograph on this page shows some specimens that I have picked up in the land. At the top is a piece of very white limestone (sedimentary rock) that comes from Jerusalem. I found it in Solomon's rock quarry under the city. The entrance is outside the walls near the Damascus Gate. Every building in Jerusalem must be faced with this stone, which gives Jerusalem a brilliant, shining appearance. Going clockwise, there is a piece of limestone from Hazor in the north and another water-tumbled piece from Achzib on the shore of the Mediterranean Sea. Below that is a specimen of copper ore from the region of Eilat in the south. Below that is a piece of rose-red sandstone from Jerash, Jordan. Similar stones can be found at Petra. Below that is a piece of conglomerate found on the fortress of Masada. At the bottom center is a piece of chert also found at Masada. At the center is a piece of blue chert from Arad in the south. Below that is a piece of flint embedded in a chalk matrix that came from Rosh ha Niqra on the Lebanon border. In the lower left corner are two pieces of basalt (lava, igneous rock) from Chorazin. They are a good indication of volcanic activity in the Galilean hills. I picked the two stones in the upper left corner out of the water of the Red Sea. Such red-colored rocks line the natural beaches of the Red Sea. They definitely give the water a reddish appearance. Wherever you are in the Holy Land, it is well to consider what you are standing on! Remember that rocks are mementos that are free.

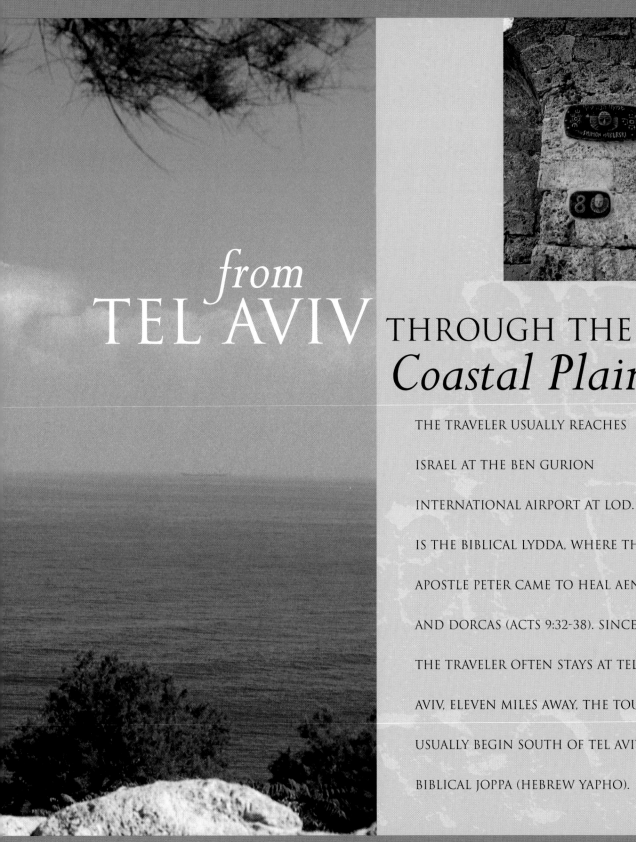

# *from* TEL AVIV

## THROUGH THE
## *Coastal Plain*

THE TRAVELER USUALLY REACHES
ISRAEL AT THE BEN GURION
INTERNATIONAL AIRPORT AT LOD. LOD
IS THE BIBLICAL LYDDA, WHERE THE
APOSTLE PETER CAME TO HEAL AENEAS
AND DORCAS (ACTS 9:32-38). SINCE
THE TRAVELER OFTEN STAYS AT TEL
AVIV, ELEVEN MILES AWAY, THE TOURS
USUALLY BEGIN SOUTH OF TEL AVIV AT
BIBLICAL JOPPA (HEBREW YAPHO).

RIGHT: *The door tile identifies the house of Simon the tanner.*

# [PART 1]
# *from* TEL AVIV
# THROUGH THE *Coastal Plain*

BELOW: *Joppa Bay has been an important seaport for thousands of years. In the conquest Joshua awarded Joppa to the tribe of Dan, but they never took the city (Josh. 19:46). King Solomon imported cedars of Lebanon for the building of the temple. They were floated down to Joppa and from there hauled up to Jerusalem (II Chron. 2:15-16). The prophet Jonah took ship at Joppa to flee from the face of the Lord (Jon. 1:3), but a great fish was waiting for him. The minaret marks the traditional house of Simon the tanner, where Peter stayed many days (Acts 9:43).*

2

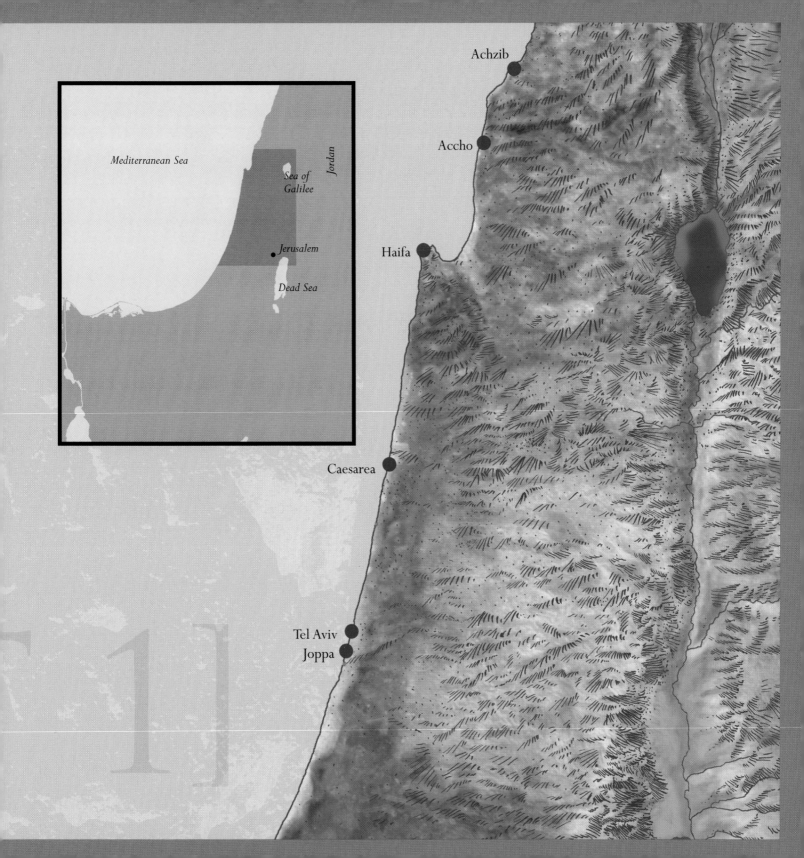

Mediterranean Sea

Sea of
Galilee

Jordan

Jerusalem

Dead Sea

Achzib

Accho

Haifa

Caesarea

Tel Aviv

Joppa

BELOW: *Today Joppa is a fishing port. The shore is lined with fishing boats. There are also excursion boats to take the traveler up and down the coast. Old Joppa was originally built on a low hill that overlooks the harbor.*

ABOVE: *Archaeological excavations at Joppa are carefully preserved and clearly labeled.*

BELOW: *On top of the hill stand the Church of St. Peter and a Franciscan monastery built to commemorate the vision that Peter had of the great sheet let down from heaven (Acts 10:9-17). That vision resulted in the conversion of Cornelius and all who were in his house (Acts 10:44-45) and began the mission to the Gentiles that the apostle Paul later took all the way to Rome.*

# JOPPA & *Tel Aviv*

ABOVE: *The first skyscraper in Tel Aviv (and in all Israel) was the twenty-five-story Shalom Tower (tower of peace). It was built on the grounds of the old Herzliya College, which had been founded in 1909. The observation deck provides this magnificent view of the modern city.*

ABOVE: *The Fredric R. Mann Auditorium is the home of the Israeli Philharmonic Orchestra.*

ABOVE: *The beautiful symmetry of the Roman arch is a good example of Roman power in building. The arch was meant to last for ages.*

RIGHT: *Traveling northward along the coast, you come to Caesarea Maritima (Caesarea by the sea), which Herod the Great built in 22-10 B.C. as his provincial capital. Philip the Evangelist came to Caesarea and remained there many years (Acts 8:40; 21:8). Peter came to Caesarea to give the Word of God to Cornelius (Acts 10:1, 24). Paul and Silas landed there on the second missionary journey (Acts 18:22). Paul was imprisoned there for two years before he made his defense before Festus (Acts 24:27–25:1-6). The walls that are standing today are Crusader walls built on top of the old Roman walls. The moat, as usual in Israel, is a dry moat. Archaeological excavations have brought a great part of Caesarea to light.*

WE THAT WERE OF PAUL'S COMPANY DEPARTED, AND CAME UNTO CAESAREA;

AND WE ENTERED INTO THE HOUSE OF PHILIP THE EVANGELIST, WHICH WAS

ONE OF THE SEVEN; AND ABODE WITH HIM.

[ACTS 21:8]

# ROMAN
## *aqueducts*

The Roman aqueduct that brought water down from Mount Carmel some twenty miles to the north is still standing. If it had not been damaged in war, it would carry water to this day.

LEFT: *If you look at the arches closely, you are liable to find a lizard looking back at you!*

# HEROD'S *Theater*

*The great theater at Caesarea has been restored and is used for modern performances. The sea breeze gives it wonderful acoustics. This is the theater in which Herod Agrippa I made his oration to the emissaries from Tyre and Sidon (Acts 12:20-21).*

RIGHT: *The excavations of Herod's palace at Caesarea have uncovered a freshwater swimming pool. There were no luxuries that he lacked.*

RIGHT: *In the theater area an inscription was found naming Pontius Pilate as the provincial governor during the reign of Tiberius Caesar. This is the only inscription known that names Pontius Pilate and is a remarkable confirmation of the historical accuracy of Luke (Luke 3:1).*

RIGHT: *Right at the shoreline in the harbor archaeologists have uncovered a temple. As soon as the ancient traveler got off the ship, he could give thanks to his god that he had made it safely to harbor.*

The Bahá'í Shrine marks the burial place of the founder of the Bahá'í faith, Bahaullah. The followers of Islam regard him as a heretic.

# Haifa

**ABOVE RIGHT:** *Haifa Bay is the only natural deep-water harbor that Israel has. It is on the northern slopes of Mount Carmel, which extends inland twelve miles from the coast. Joshua conquered Carmel and gave it to the tribe of Asher (Josh. 12:22; 19:26). Elijah had a powerful ministry on Mount Carmel (I Kings 18:19-42). The prophets referred to Carmel as a fruitful place (Jer. 50:19; Mic. 7:14). The golden dome of the Baha'i Shrine is at the lower left. The Jews call the massive grain storehouse at the shore "Dagon" after the name of the Philistine god of grain.*

**RIGHT:** *There are magnificent gardens surrounding the shrine. This jacaranda tree has a bougainvillea vine growing all through it, mixing the colors of the blossoms.*

**LEFT:** *Pomegranates grow well on Mount Carmel. The pomegranate blooms for a long season so that there are buds, flowers, and fruit all on the same tree. The Lord promised the Israelites pomegranates in the Holy Land (Deut. 8:8). The robes of the high priest were adorned with golden bells and pomegranates (Exod. 28:33-34).*

ABOVE: *Models of ancient vessels fill the museum.*

ABOVE: *Actual storage jars found in shipwrecks at the bottom of the Mediterranean are on display.*

RIGHT: *The National Maritime Museum in Haifa has fascinating displays of underwater archaeology.*

LEFT: *Across the bay from Haifa is the city of Accho (in the New Testament Ptolemais). The Israelites were unable to drive out the inhabitants of Accho (Judg. 1:31). Paul and his company came to Ptolemais on his return to Jerusalem (Acts 21:7).*

*Haifa Bay is a beautiful sight at night.*

LEFT: *On one trip we stayed at the Dan Carmel Hotel. The lower-cost rooms were all filled, so they put me, as tour leader, in the presidential suite on the top floor just because it was empty. At dinner I invited the group to bring tripods and cameras to get a magnificent view from the balcony of Haifa Bay at night. As the group streamed in to get pictures, a Jewish man followed them in and watched them take photos, chatting with members of the tour. On his way out he turned to me and said, "All I can say is that I'm sure glad I'm not paying for this place." I did not have the heart to tell him that I wasn't either!*

TOP: *On the Accho side of the bay fishing boats dominate the shore.*

ABOVE: *The bazaar in Accho is a good place to find fresh fish. The old saying is "Need one bring fish to Accho?"*

RIGHT: *The old walls of Accho are built upon even older walls.*

RIGHT: *The Turkish Inn at Accho is a good example of a caravanserai. The tower, however, was built in the nineteenth century.*

# Accho

The court of the inn is no doubt similar to the inn that the Holy Family sought at Bethlehem (Luke 2:7). The animals were stabled in the lower arch, and the travelers stayed in the upper part. The only convenience furnished was the well in the center of the court. But even in a Spartan place like this, there was no room for the Lord Jesus.

BELOW LEFT: *Achzib, a city nineteen miles north of Accho, was given to the tribe of Asher (Josh. 19:29), but they did not drive out the inhabitants (Judg. 1:31). There is a millstone at Achzib that is a striking example of one of the Lord's illustrations. The Lord Jesus, referring to one who would offend one of those little ones who believe in Him, said it would be better that a "millstone were hanged about his neck" and he be drowned in the depths of the sea (Matt. 18:6). A person would certainly go down abruptly if he had a stone of that size around his neck!* BELOW RIGHT: *The guesthouse at Shavei Zion (homecomers to Zion) is a modern motel. Refugees from Hitler's persecution established a moshav (a type of kibbutz), which is a collective farm. The main cash crop is cut flowers, which are airlifted to the capitals of Europe.*

LEFT: *Near the shore is a mosaic floor from an old Christian church.*

# THE TOWN OF *Achzib*

From the ruins of Achzib one can look northward to the chalk cliffs of Rosh ha Niqra (the Cape of the Grotto) at the Lebanon border. The cliffs are the southern tip of a series of hills in Lebanon that are called the "Ladder of Tyre."

RIGHT: *There are cable cars to take travelers down to the base of the chalk cliffs to see the network of caves that the Mediterranean has worn in the cliff.*

*the*
# GROTTO

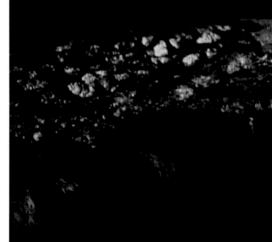

LEFT: *The strong currents have carved many caves out of the soft chalk cliffs. There are paved walkways into a number of caves.*

The largest cave is called the Grotto.
It is exciting to stand in the darkened
cave and hear the waves booming in
and out, still carving the rock.

# ACROSS THE
# *Galilean Hills*

NOW IT IS TIME TO LEAVE THE
COASTAL REGION AND TRAVEL
THROUGH THE GALILEAN HILLS.
THEY ARE ACTUALLY A SOUTHERN
EXTENSION OF THE FOOTHILLS OF
THE LEBANON AND ANTI-LEBANON
MOUNTAIN RANGES IN LEBANON.
MOUNT HERMON IS THE POINT AT
WHICH THE BORDERS OF ISRAEL,
LEBANON, AND SYRIA MEET.

[PART 2]
# ACROSS THE
# *Galilean Hills*

ABOVE RIGHT: *A site rarely visited is the Crusader castle Montfort, built by the Teutonic knights in A.D. 1226. It is built on the spur of a hill with a sheer drop on three sides and a whole series of walls and towers on the access side. When enemy troops approached, it would take an hour to scale the slopes to the formidable castle.*

BELOW: *From the top of the tel the route of the Via Maris is obvious. There is a commanding view of the countryside.*

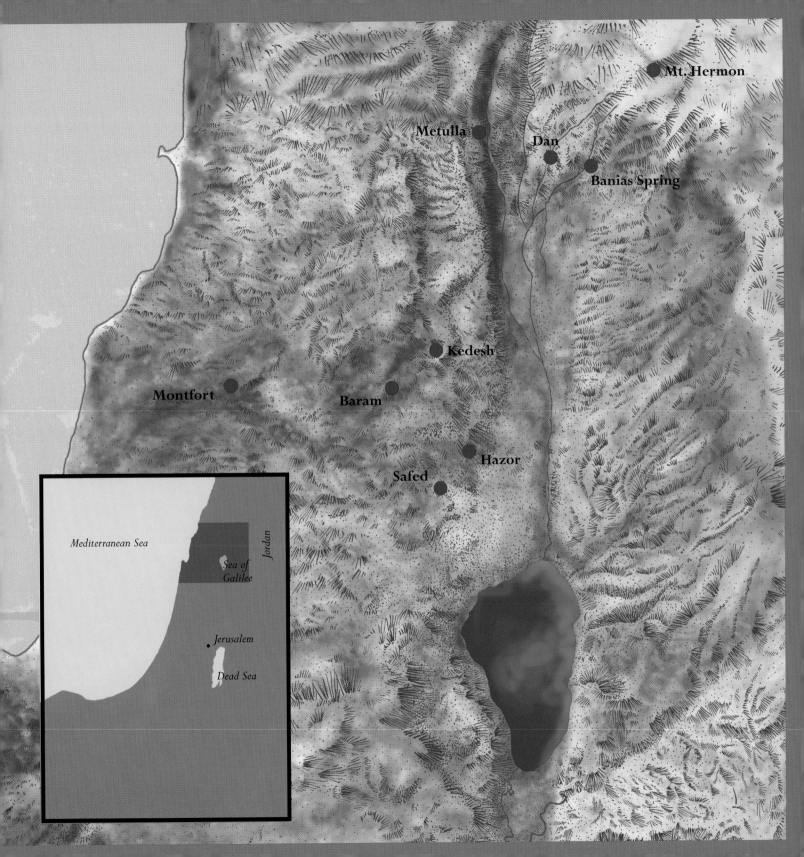

Mt. Hermon

Metulla

Dan

Baniás Spring

Kedesh

Montfort

Baram

Hazor

Safed

*Mediterranean Sea*

*Jordan*

*Sea of Galilee*

• *Jerusalem*

*Dead Sea*

*The ancient synagogue at Baram is well preserved. It is very close to the Lebanon border.*

**ABOVE:** *The tel of Kedesh Naphtali awaits the archaeologist's pick. A tel is a man-made hill formed like a layer cake. The city was built and destroyed, rebuilt and destroyed, each layer raising the height of the mound. Kedesh was conquered by Joshua and made into one of the six cities of refuge (Josh. 12:22; 20:7). Deborah summoned Barak from Kedesh (Judg. 4:6). Tiglath-pileser finally destroyed it and deported the inhabitants to Assyria (II Kings 15:29).*

**LEFT:** *Metulla is a small town on the Lebanon border. It is the northernmost settlement in Israel and has been a crossing point for many south Lebanese who work in Israel.*

**BELOW:** *Montfort is an impressive Crusader castle. It can be reached only on foot.*

תירות
אוצר לאומי
MINISTRY OF TOURISM
& MUNICIPALITY OF METULLA
*Welcome you!*

Traveling farther to the northeast, one comes to Caesarea Philippi, where the Banias Spring flows from a mighty cliff. This is the place where the apostle Peter made his great confession of the Lord, "Thou art the Christ, the Son of the living God" (Matt. 16:16). These words are especially significant in view of the impressive setting, with living water pouring from the rock. The Banias Spring is the second of the sources of the Jordan River. (The third source is the Hatsbani River, which flows in from Lebanon.)

LEFT: *While climbing around the rocks, one may be fortunate enough to see a coney (a Syrian rock hyrax). It looks like a rabbit without the ears but is no relation to the rabbit. The coney is well known for taking refuge in the rocks (Ps. 104:18). "The conies are but a feeble folk, yet make they their houses in the rocks" (Prov. 30:26).*

# BANIAS *Spring*

TOP: *Near the spring are caves and shrines carved in the rock, dedicated to the Greek god Pan. The place was formerly known as Panias Spring.*

ABOVE: *Mount Hermon dominates the whole northeastern part of the land. At 9,232 feet, it is the highest mountain of Israel (and of Syria as well). It is the southernmost peak of the Anti-Lebanon range. Even in summer there is snow at the pinnacle. In winter ski slopes are in operation.*

RIGHT: *On the slopes of Mount Hermon is a beautiful lake in the crater of an extinct volcano. It is called Berekhat Ram, "the high pool." It is formed by snowmelt and springs in Hermon.*

AS THE DEW OF HERMON, AND AS THE DEW THAT DESCENDED

UPON THE MOUNTAINS OF ZION: FOR THERE THE LORD

COMMANDED THE BLESSING, MT. HERMON

EVEN LIFE FOR EVERMORE.

[PSALM 133:3]

BELOW: *The closer you come to the mountain, the more impressive it seems. Scripture likens the dew of Hermon to the blessing of God (Ps. 133:3).*

RIGHT: *The city of Hazor is another tel that dominates the countryside. The traveler approaches Hazor along the Via Maris, the ancient trade route between Damascus and Egypt. Hazor was in a position to levy tolls on the merchants that passed by. The tel, the largest in northern Israel, covers 225 acres. No wonder that Hazor was the head over all the northern part of Israel (Josh. 11:10-11). It was the only city in the north that Joshua burned (Josh. 11:13). It finally fell to Tiglath-pileser, who carried the captives of Hazor to Assyria (II Kings 15:29).*

# HAZOR

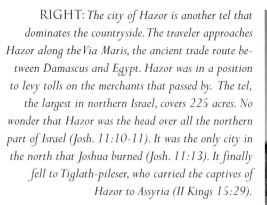

*The archaeologist Yigael Yadin found the great well that was the water source for the city. It was not a spring. Every housewife in Hazor had to walk down to the water level and carry back up every pot of water she used.*

LEFT: *Yadin also found the Solomonic gate. It had a distinctive form of three guard chambers on each side of the passage. Solomon is said to have built three cities in Israel: Hazor, Megiddo, and Gezer (I Kings 9:15). That distinctive gate has been found in each of them, and in those three cities alone. This is certainly a great confirmation of the accuracy of the Bible.*

LEFT: *Excavations have uncovered walls from the Israelite period.*

*From the top of the tel the route of the Via Maris is obvious. There is a commanding view of the countryside.*

# HAZOR
## *Museum*

TOP: *An archaeological museum at Hazor displays many of the artifacts found on the tel.*

RIGHT: *A great storage jar has been reassembled like a jigsaw puzzle. Such jars were not flat on the bottom, but rounded, to be sunk in the ground.*

LEFT: *In one of the cases are Baal, "lord," the bull god, and Ashtoreth, the female deity (Judg. 2:13; I Kings 11:33).*

BELOW: *There is also a display of the standing stones, a shrine found at Hazor. One stone is carved with upraised hands toward the moon goddess sign. These are replicas; the originals are in the Israel Museum at Jerusalem.*

*Galilee is famous for its ancient olive trees. The olive never gets very tall, but when it dies, the root resprouts, and the trunk keeps getting larger. This one has been there for many centuries.*

BELOW: *This is the small synagogue of Rabbi Joseph Caro, who died in* A.D. *1757.*

BELOW LEFT: *Here is a rare sight in Galilee, a tomb with the rolling stone still in place.*

RIGHT: *The famous rabbinic city of Safed is also in the Galilean hills. Safed is well known for its synagogues. The Orthodox congregation always faces the great ark in which the scrolls of the Torah (the Law) are kept, covered with brocade. Note the lectern. The rabbi turns his back on the congregation to read the sacred scrolls.*

# AROUND the *Sea* of GALILEE

THE SEA OF GALILEE IS CALLED THE SEA OF CHINNERETH (JOSH. 13:27), THE LAKE OF GENNESARET (LUKE 5:1), AND THE SEA OF TIBERIAS (JOHN 6:1) AS WELL. IT IS ABOUT 685 FEET BELOW SEA LEVEL BUT HAS SEASONAL FLUCTUATIONS. BETHSAIDA (MATT. 11:21), WHICH IS ON THE NORTH SIDE OF THE SEA, HAS BEEN RECENTLY EXCAVATED.

# AROUND the *Sea* of GALILEE

TOP: *The Sea of Galilee at dawn. On every trip I rise at 4 to 5 A.M. to set up a tripod to get sunrise pictures. Most of the time I get a dull gray morning. One morning I overslept and awoke to see light streaming in the window. I grabbed the camera, rushed to the window, and got the most colorful photo I ever took without leaving the hotel room!*

ABOVE: *At any time the Sea of Galilee is a lovely sight. This is a view from the shore of the kibbutz Nof Ginosar, where the Galilee boat was found.*

Chorazin

Bethsaida

Mt. of the Beatitudes

Capernaum

Tabgha

Tiberias

Ein Gev

Mediterranean Sea

Jordan

Sea of Galilee

•Jerusalem

Dead Sea

RIGHT: *This painfully small house at Chorazin has been rebuilt. The white line across the wall marks the archaeologist's work. Below the line the wall was found* in situ, *that is, in place. Above the line they have refitted the stones back into place.*

# *Chorazin* &
# CAPERNAUM

*The synagogue at Chorazin. Chorazin, about two miles from Galilee, is one of the towns that the Lord Jesus pronounced a curse upon (Matt. 11:21; Luke 10:13). The synagogue was built from the local black basalt stone. It has been partially reconstructed.*

*This synagogue was the site of the Lord's message on the bread of life (John 6:24-59). Capernaum was also the place where the Lord healed the centurion's servant (Matt. 8:5-13).*

FAR LEFT: *At Capernaum there is a beautiful white stone synagogue that is undoubtedly the place in which the Lord Jesus ministered (Mark 1:21). Note that the white stone is resting on a previous black stone foundation, which was the original synagogue at Capernaum. When a synagogue became too old to use, the Jews would not just move across the street to build another. They would raze the building and rebuild it on the same consecrated ground. Thus, that synagogue is one place in which you can know that you walked where Jesus walked.*

ABOVE: *The stones of the synagogue have characteristic Jewish symbols, such as the star of David.*

# CHURCH
## OF THE
# *Beatitudes*

*The balcony of the Church of the Beatitudes provides a lovely view of the Sea of Galilee. We often hold church services here on the balcony.*

TOP: *Not far from Capernaum is the traditional Mount of the Beatitudes, where a beautiful Franciscan chapel overlooks the shore of Galilee. This is the most likely site of the Sermon on the Mount (Matt. 5-7).*

ABOVE: *In the chapel, stained glass windows record each of the eight Beatitudes.*

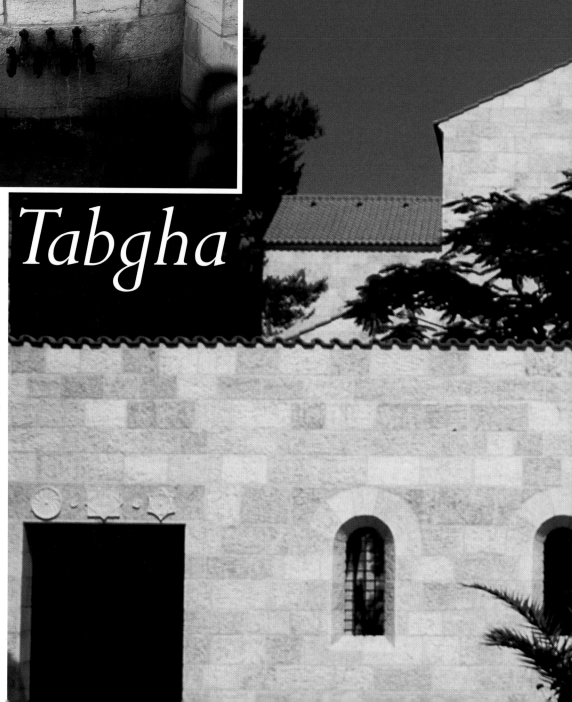

# Tabgha

ABOVE: *Just south of the Mount of the Beatitudes is Tabgha, the ancient Magdala, the town from which Mary Magdalene came (Matt. 27:56; Luke 8:2). Tabgha is an Arabic contraction of the Greek Heptapegon, "seven springs," which still flow forth through pipes.*

RIGHT: *Near the springs is the Church of the Multiplication of the Loaves and Fishes. It commemorates the feeding of the five thousand (Matt. 14:15-21). Although the church is of recent construction, its design is in the style of the fifth century Byzantine basilica. The mosaic floor is indeed ancient and is often called the most beautiful in all Israel.*

BELOW: *At the altar of the church is the mosaic of the loaves and fishes. The loaves are hot cross buns! There are many birds and animals portrayed on the floor.*

BOTTOM: *The gardens in the area have passion-flower vines in them.*

47

# TIBERIAS

RIGHT: *Farther down the western shore of Galilee is the city of Tiberias, the center of commerce and communications for Galilee. The city was founded in A.D. 20 by Herod Antipas and has had a long history as a center of rabbinic learning. The New Testament mentions boats that came from Tiberias (John 6:23). This scene from the hilltop has not changed much in the past two thousand years.*

RIGHT: *The view toward the city of Tiberias, however, is constantly changing as the city expands.*

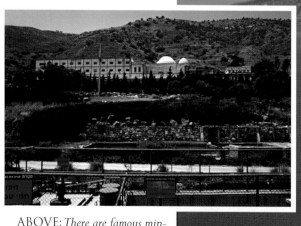

ABOVE: *There are famous mineral springs and health spas in Tiberias, as this scene shows. In the center are the ruins of the ancient synagogue at Tiberias. Above are the twin domes of the tomb of Rabbi Meir.*

ABOVE: *The mosaic floor of the synagogue shows the ark in which the scrolls of the law were kept, flanked by a menorah (a seven-branched lamp stand) on each side. The black basalt stone is typical of natural stone in the area.*

LEFT: *North of Tiberias are hills called the Horns of Hattin, site of a major battle during the Crusades.*

# TIBERIAS

ABOVE: *A modern-day synagogue at the kib-butz Lavi, a few miles west of Tiberias, shows the ark that held the scrolls with lamps on each side. The people of the kibbutz built the synagogue as a replica of one in Europe de-stroyed by the Nazi persecution.*

RIGHT: *Inside the ark are the Torah scrolls in silver cases.*

*The jacaranda trees are a lovely sight in Tiberias.*

ABOVE: *In Tiberias is the tomb of the famous rabbi Yohanan ben Zakkai, who lived at the time of the destruction of Jerusalem in A.D. 70. The Lord Jesus used such tombs as an illustration of the sin of hypocrisy. He denounced the super-pious scribes as whitewashed sepulchres, which are beautiful outwardly but within are full of dead men's bones (Matt. 23:27).*

*In the synagogue area in Tiberias there are spikenard bushes. The fragrance is mentioned in Song of Solomon 1:12. Mary brought a pound of spikenard ointment to anoint the feet of Jesus (John 12:3).*

ABOVE: *Large resort hotels are now springing up along the shore of Tiberias.*

BELOW: *One of the highlights of any visit to the Holy Land is a boat ride in a large motor launch across the Sea of Galilee. Since the widest part of Galilee is only seven to eight miles across, it is a short trip to the kibbutz Ein Gev on the eastern side.*

# EIN GEV

RIGHT: *The conical hill behind Ein Gev is Sussita, the ancient Hippos.*

*A royal poinciana tree (flame tree) is a beautiful sight at Ein Gev*

LEFT: *Among the many artifacts displayed at Ein Gev are a number of stone anchors that were used by ancient boatmen on Galilee.*

FAR LEFT: *Along the shore there is a war memorial for those who died in 1948: the widow and the child.*

LEFT: *A stone hollowed out for an aqueduct is another display.*

# GADARA
## &THE Jordan River

TOP: *The church faces the Sea of Galilee from a distance.*    LEFT: *Driving north from Ein Gev you come to the early church that commemorates the Lord's deliverance of the Gadarene demoniac (Luke 8:26-39). There is good evidence for thinking that this is the correct site. It is the only place that has a cliff along the shore. (See John McRay,* Archaeology and the New Testament, *pp. 166-68.)*

TOP: *At the southern tip of the Sea of Galilee the waters flow forth into the Jordan River. This is the Jordan at its widest and most beautiful.*
ABOVE, INSET: *Israel has constructed a place for baptism with a concrete ramp and strong railings. Some Christians wish to be rebaptized in the Jordan River.* ABOVE: *When the Jordan nears the Dead Sea at the Allenby Bridge, it is a poor, muddy stream barely ten feet wide. Evaporation and irrigation take their toll.*

ABOVE: *As the Jordan flows southward, it meanders through an ever-deepening valley with the hills of Jordan on the eastern side and the hills of Samaria on the western side.*

# *from* GALILEE *to* Jerusalem

THE ORIGIN OF SAMARIA AS A COUN-

TRY GOES BACK TO THE REVOLT OF

JEROBOAM AGAINST REHOBOAM, WHICH

FORMED THE NORTHERN KINGDOM OF

ISRAEL (I KINGS 11:26-31; 12:16-24). BOTH

ISRAEL AND JUDAH WERE TAKEN INTO

CAPTIVITY AS A DIVINE JUDGMENT FOR

SIN (II KINGS 17:4-8; 25:1-9). A REMNANT

RETURNED FROM BOTH DEPORTATIONS

(II KINGS 17:24-41; EZRA 2:1). BY THE TIME

OF JESUS THE JEWS HAD NO DEALINGS

WITH THE SAMARITANS (JOHN 4:9).

TOP RIGHT: *It is not far from the Sea of Galilee to BelVoir, the mighty Crusader castle. But BelVoir is built on the high Samaritan hills overlooking the Jordan valley. The defenders had a commanding view of any troop movements.*

BOTTOM RIGHT: *The view southward is a twenty-mile sweep of the Jordan valley. No wonder they named it BelVoir (beautiful view).*

*from*

# GALILEE

*to*

# Jerusalem

[PART 4]

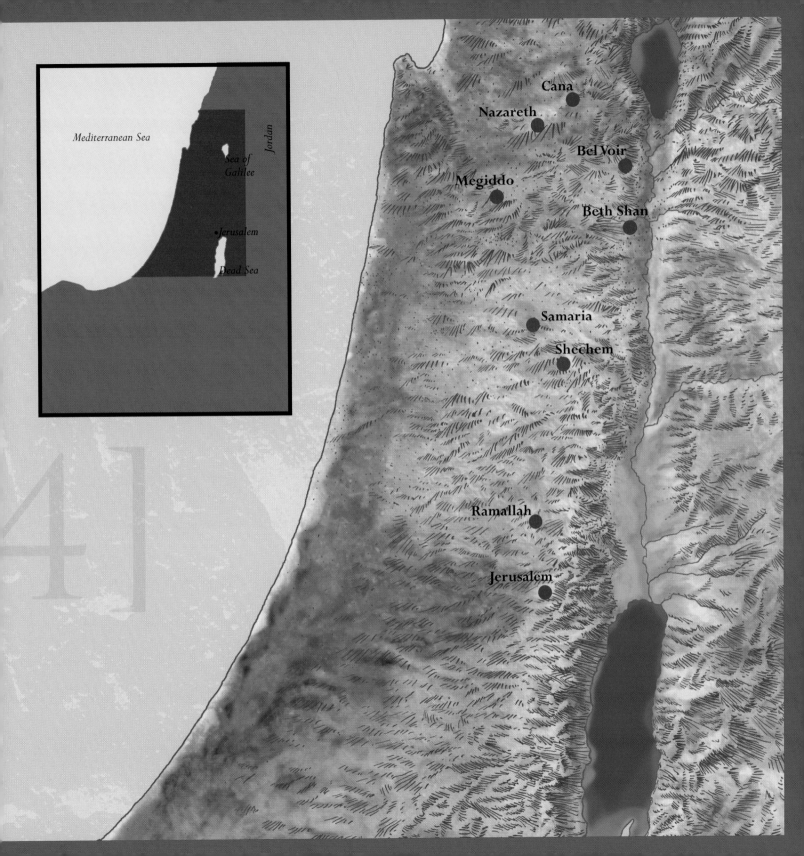

Mediterranean Sea

Sea of Galilee

Jordan

•Jerusalem

Dead Sea

Cana

Nazareth

Bel Voir

Megiddo

Beth Shan

Samaria

Shechem

Ramallah

Jerusalem

LEFT: *Colonnaded street restored at Beth Shan.*

*Farther south is Beth Shan, a city of Manasseh (Josh. 17:11). But the Israelites did not drive out the inhabitants of Beth Shan (Judg. 1:27). The Philistines put the bodies of King Saul and his sons on the wall of Beth Shan (I Sam. 31:10). The tel was the Old Testament city; the excavations in the foreground are the Roman and Byzantine city.*

# *Beth*SHAN

BELOW: *View of Beth Shan from the tel.*

BELOW: *The city street and pillars are the center of the Roman city. Beth Shan is the best-preserved Roman city in the Holy Land.*

RIGHT: *The Roman theater has been partially restored.*

BELOW: *Beth Shan is the largest Roman city to be excavated in Israel. Jerash is larger, but it is in Jordan.*

# *Beth* SHAN

*The roof of the Roman bath being reconstructed.*

*The hill of Moreh stretches out like a pointing finger. The town at the foot of Moreh is Nain, where the Lord Jesus restored the son of the widow of Nain (Luke 7:11-16).*

# Valley of ARMAGEDDON

RIGHT: *Traveling westward into the valley of Armageddon, you come to Gideon's spring at the foot of Mount Gilboa. It is called the well of Harod, south of the hill of Moreh (Judg. 7:1).*

BELOW: *Mount Tabor is a conical hill to which Deborah and Barak gathered their forces and then came down to defeat the army of Sisera (Judg. 4:12-14). It is a wild ride up the switchbacks by taxi to get to the top.*

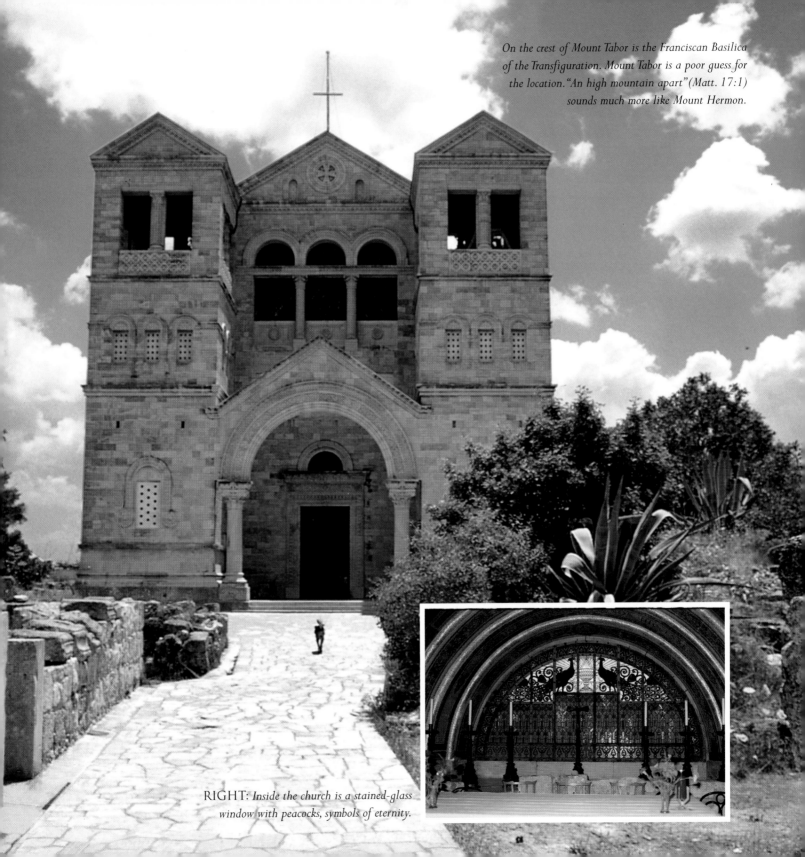

On the crest of Mount Tabor is the Franciscan Basilica of the Transfiguration. Mount Tabor is a poor guess for the location. "An high mountain apart" (Matt. 17:1) sounds much more like Mount Hermon.

RIGHT: Inside the church is a stained-glass window with peacocks, symbols of eternity.

# Nazareth

ABOVE: *The city of Nazareth is built on the crest, which is the southern part of the Galilean hills. At Nazareth the angel revealed to Mary the coming birth of the Lord (Luke 1:26-38). This was the boyhood home of the Lord Jesus (Matt. 2:23; 4:13). He was known as "Jesus of Nazareth"(Matt. 26:71).*

BELOW: *Toward the north of the valley of Armageddon is the Nazareth escarpment, the Mount of the Precipitation.*

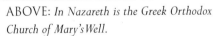

ABOVE: *In Nazareth is the Greek Orthodox Church of Mary's Well.*

LEFT: *The well, now in the church, was the only water source for Nazareth.*

CENTER: *When the mob led the Lord out to the brow of the hill (the Mount of the Precipitation), it was to an eight-hundred-foot drop (Luke 4:16-29).*

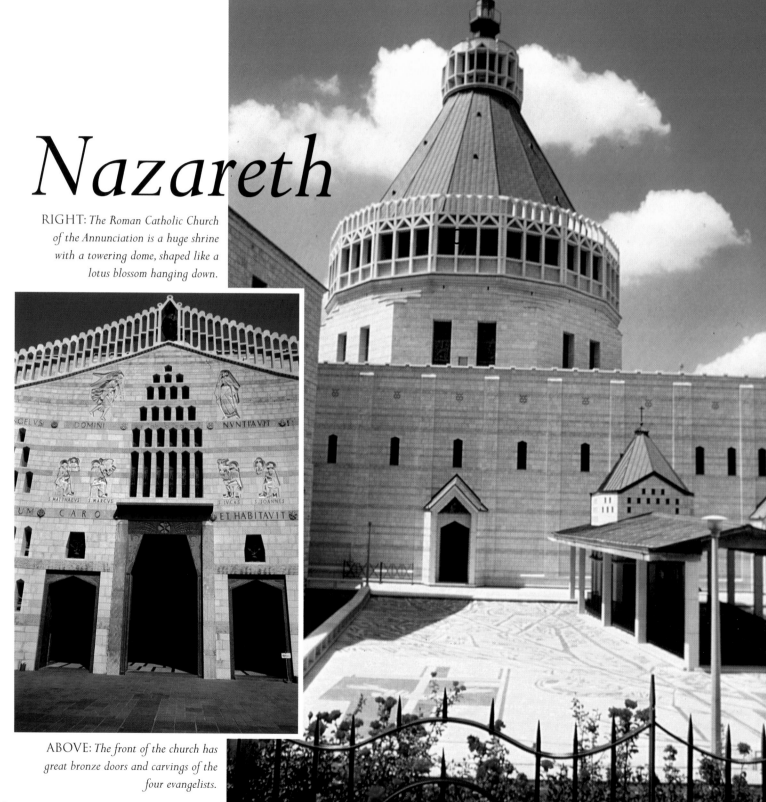

# Nazareth

RIGHT: *The Roman Catholic Church of the Annunciation is a huge shrine with a towering dome, shaped like a lotus blossom hanging down.*

ABOVE: *The front of the church has great bronze doors and carvings of the four evangelists.*

# CANA

LEFT: *Just north of Nazareth is Cana, a wide spot in the road. To help a poor couple at a wedding banquet, the Lord Jesus turned water into wine (John 2:1-11). A Catholic church memorializes the miracle.*

LEFT: *Inside the church a large stone water pot accurately shows the size of the pots.*

BELOW: *Kishon flows alongside Mount Carmel all the way to the sea. When Deborah and Barak fought Sisera, rain caused the Kishon to overflow, miring Sisera's chariots (Judg. 5:7-22). Elijah brought the priests of Baal to the Kishon to execute them (I Kings 18:40).*

RIGHT: *At the southwestern corner of the valley of Armageddon stands the tel of Megiddo, which guards the pass between the mountains of Samaria and Mount Carmel. There is a long history of war at Megiddo. Although Joshua defeated the king of Megiddo (Josh. 12:21), the Canaanites continued dwelling there (Judg. 1:27). Pharaoh-nechoh slew King Josiah at Megiddo (II Kings 23:29-30).*

# MEGIDDO

ABOVE: *Looking down from the top of the tel of Megiddo, one can see the reason for the importance of Megiddo. There was a vital crossroad there. The great Via Maris, the way of the sea, ran from Damascus to Egypt, passing Megiddo. But the way of the mountains ran from Samaria to Accho, right past Megiddo. Whoever held Megiddo had a stranglehold on transportation and communication in the land. Thus, armies have fought at Megiddo over and over. There is yet another battle to be fought there. The future Antichrist will bring his forces to Megiddo to crush the Jews and all others into submission at the mount of Megiddo (Rev. 16:14-16).*

# MEGIDDO

BELOW: *In the Canaanite level at Megiddo archaeologists found a great altar.*

BELOW: *This gate is very distinctive: three guard chambers on each side of a central passageway. The historical sign in front of the gate shows the diagram clearly. Solomon built these walls of Megiddo, as he did those of Hazor and Gezer (I Kings 9:15). Only in these three cities has the Solomonic gate been found.*

RIGHT: *The tunnel leads under the wall of the city to a spring, which was carefully hidden from the outside so that besieging armies could not discover the water source.*

*Inside Megiddo are steps that lead down to a tunnel.*

The massive walls of the city of Samaria show that it was the capital of the northern kingdom of Omri and Ahab (I Kings 16:24-29). It was built on a three hundred-foot-high hill only nineteen miles from the Mediterranean coast, close to pagan influence. It took the Assyrians a three-year siege to break the power of Samaria and take it captive (II Kings 17:5-6).

LEFT: *All that is left of Ahab's palace is a pile of ruins. One can still find flecks of ivory among the stones of the walls (I Kings 22:39).*

# SAMARIA

BELOW LEFT: *Traveling farther south, you come to the modern town of Nablus. Looking northward, you can see Mount Ebal, remarkable for its desolation. There is not a tree on it. Mount Ebal was the place from which the curses of the law were read (Deut. 27:13; 28:15-68).*

BELOW RIGHT: *Toward the south lies Mount Gerizim, from which the blessings of the law were read (Deut. 27:12; 28:1-14). Gerizim is lush and green with trees. The Samaritans claim Mount Gerizim for their home.*

RIGHT: *Jacob's well is not far away. It is found underground in an unfinished church. This is the place that the Lord Jesus spoke to the woman of Samaria at the well (John 4:5-26).*

BELOW: *Hollyhocks grow wild along the road.*

ABOVE: *The ancient city of Shechem lies between Ebal and Gerizim. It is easy to find the*

# Nearing JERUSALEM

*city gate, which is very different from the Solomonic gates. There are twin stones at each of the gate corners. Shechem was the first place in which Abraham built an altar to the Lord in the land (Gen. 12:6-7). Jacob's family buried their strange gods in Shechem (Gen. 35:4). Shechem was one of the six cities of refuge (Josh. 20:7). Rehoboam was crowned king there (I Kings 12:1). After the revolt, Jeroboam rebuilt Shechem and lived there (I Kings 12:25).*

Thirty miles north of Jerusalem is the modern
city of Ramallah, which is near the ancient city of Ramah,
home of the prophet Samuel (I Sam. 28:3). Near Ramallah an unimproved
road turns off toward the west. It seems impossibly narrow for a tour bus. Down that road is
a small Arab village and the great well at Gibeon. This was the place where Joab and Abner met with their troops
(II Sam. 2:12-17). The contest turned into civil war, which Joab's men won. The well is now filled in, but the steps
originally led all the way down to the water level.

# AROUND *Jerusalem*

THE MOST IMPRESSIVE APPROACH TO JERUSALEM IS FROM THE NORTHEAST ON THE MOUNT OF OLIVES ROAD OVER MOUNT SCOPUS. MOUNT SCOPUS WAS THE PLACE IN WHICH TITUS AND THE ROMAN LEGIONS CAMPED IN THE SIEGE OF JERUSALEM. THE CRUSADERS ALSO CAMPED HERE IN A.D. 1099— MANY OF THEM MOVED TO TEARS BY THE FIRST SIGHT OF THE HOLY CITY.

ABOVE: *The overview of Jerusalem from Mount Scopus provides a lovely sight. There are well-landscaped observation points.*

# AROUND Jerusalem [PART 5]

ABOVE: *The original campus of the Hebrew University is located on Mount Scopus.*

Mount
Scopus

Hebrew
University

Church of the
Holy Trinity

Rockefeller
Museum

Garden Tomb

Mount of
Olives

Herod's
Gate

Damascus
Gate

Lions'
Gate

Church of
All Nations

Church of
the Ascension

New
Gate

Golden
Gate

The Knesset

Jaffa
Gate

Absalom's
Tomb

Pater Noster
Church

Dung
Gate

YMCA

Hill of
Ophel

Dominus Flevit

Zion
Gate

Kidron Valley

Church of
Mary Magdalene

Tomb of
David

St. Peter
Gallicantu

Pool of
Siloam

Farther south is the Roman Catholic Church of the Ascension,
now in Muslim hands. There are holes in the rock, supposedly
left by the Lord's feet as He ascended.

# Olivet CHURCHES

ILONGO

FRANÇAIS

ESPERANTO

Notre Père qui es
aux cieux que ton nom
soit sanctifié; que ton
règne vienne; que ta
volonté soit faite sur la
terre comme au ciel donne
nous aujourd'hui notre pain
de ce jour; pardonne-nous
nos offenses comme nous
pardonnons aussi à ceux
qui nous ont offensés
et ne nous soûmets pas à
la tentation; mais délivre
nous du Mal.
Amen.
Pâques 1966

Patro nia, kiu estas
en la cielo. Sanktig-
ata estu via nomo.
Venu via regno. Fa-
rigu via volo, ki-
el en la cielo, tiel
ankaŭ sur la tero.
Nian panon ĉiutag-
an donu al ni hod-
iaŭ. Kaj pardonu al
ni niajn suldojn,
kiel ankaŭ ni pardo
nasal niaj ŝuldantoj.
Kaj ne konduku nin en
tenton. Sed liberigu nin
de la malbono.
Amen.

LATIN

PATER noster; qui
es in cœlis, sanctifi-
cetur nomen tuum; ad-
veniat regnum tuum.
Fiat voluntas tua sicut
in cœlo et in terra.
Panem nostrum super-
substantialem da no-
bis hodiè. Et dimitte
nobis debita nostra,
sicut et nos dimitti-
mus debitoribus nos-
tris. Et ne nos inducas
in tentationem; sed li-
bera nos à malo.
Amen.

TOP: *Nearby is the Pater Noster Church, dedicated to the Lord's Prayer (Matt. 6:9-13). There are over 150 translations of the Lord's Prayer set as majolica tiles in the walls of the church and the cloister. Ilongo, French, and Esperanto are some of the languages. New translations are constantly being added.*

ABOVE: *The gate of Pater Noster is adorned with climbing roses.*

LEFT: *The church gets its name from the first two words of the Latin translation of the Lord's Prayer.*

83

ABOVE: *Down the slope of the Mount of Olives is the Church Dominus Flevit, "The Lord wept," which commemorates the Lord's tears over Jerusalem (Luke 19:41-42). The church, on the right side of the picture, looks across the Kidron Valley toward the Dome of the Rock.*

BELOW: *Dominus Flevit has what is undoubtedly the most famous window in Jerusalem. It is deeply moving to sit in that small church and look out through that window on the Holy City.*

*Coming down to the Kidron Valley and beginning at the northeastern corner of the city, the Rockefeller Museum is just across the street.*

This is an exact reconstruction of a Hyksos tomb just as it was found.

ABOVE LEFT: *A horned altar from Megiddo is on display. The horns of the altar are often mentioned in Scripture (Exod. 29:12; Lev. 4:7; I Kings 1:50-51).*

ABOVE: *Huge storage jars are everywhere in the museum.*

LEFT: *Cases display ancient gold jewelry found in excavations.*

LEFT: *An Egyptian stele with hieroglyphs (in white) records the first mention of the nation Israel in history.*

ABOVE: *On Thursdays (before the Muslim holy day, Friday) you can find the sheep market at the Stork Tower on the Kidron side.*

LEFT: *Just north of the temple area is St. Stephen's Gate, often called the Lions' Gate from the pair of carved lions on each side. It is the closest gate to the place of Stephen's martyrdom (Acts 7:57-60).*

ABOVE: *The Stork Tower is the northeastern corner of the Old City of Jerusalem, called this because storks used to nest on the top.*

O JERUSALEM, JERUSALEM, . . . HOW OFTEN WOULD I HAVE GATHERED THY
CHILDREN TOGETHER . . . AND YE WOULD NOT!          [MATT. 23:37]

# Gethsemane

RIGHT: *The old olive trees in Gethsemane stand only about twenty feet tall, but their bases are six to eight feet across at ground level. When an olive tree dies, it may resprout. These trees may be the same roots of first-century trees. One would have to cut them down and count the rings to prove it. The leaves of the olive are a silvery gray green. Somewhere near these trees the Lord Jesus came to pray on that last night before the cruci-fixion (Matt. 26:36-46).*

BELOW: *From the Garden of Gethsemane one can look up at the walled-up Golden Gate through the bougainvillea.*

ABOVE: *Farther south along the Kidron Valley brings you to the Church of All Nations at Gethsemane, seen from the walls of Jerusalem. The Garden of Gethsemane is just to the left of the church (Matt. 26:36-46).*

LEFT: *The front façade of the church is very distinctive. There are stags on each side of the cross. Statues of the four evangelists stand on the pillars.*

# *Valley of* KIDRON

RIGHT: *Not far from Gethsemane is the Russian Orthodox Church of St. Mary Magdalene.*

BELOW: *Still farther down the Kidron Valley is the Pillar of Absalom, which probably dates from one thousand years after Absalom! The Grotto of St. James has pillars in it; the Tomb of Zechariah has a top like a pyramid. These are merely popular names for old monuments.*

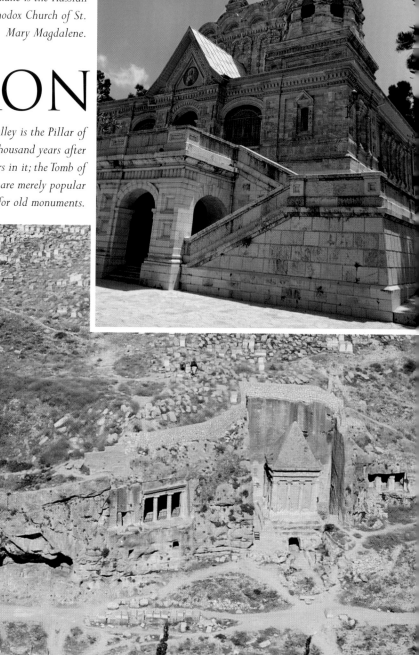

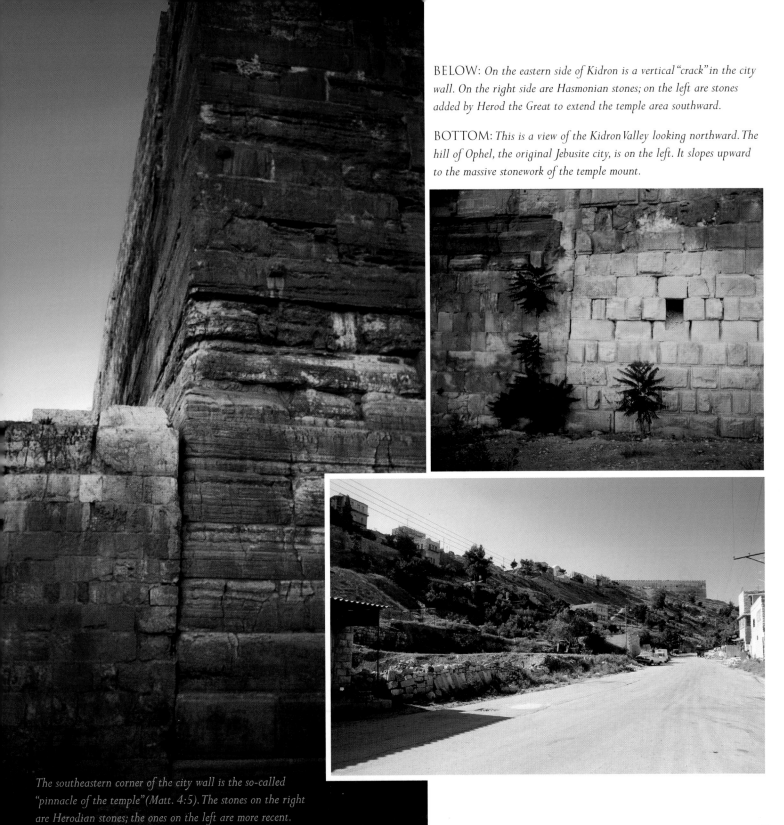

BELOW: *On the eastern side of Kidron is a vertical "crack" in the city wall. On the right side are Hasmonian stones; on the left are stones added by Herod the Great to extend the temple area southward.*

BOTTOM: *This is a view of the Kidron Valley looking northward. The hill of Ophel, the original Jebusite city, is on the left. It slopes upward to the massive stonework of the temple mount.*

*The southeastern corner of the city wall is the so-called "pinnacle of the temple" (Matt. 4:5). The stones on the right are Herodian stones; the ones on the left are more recent.*

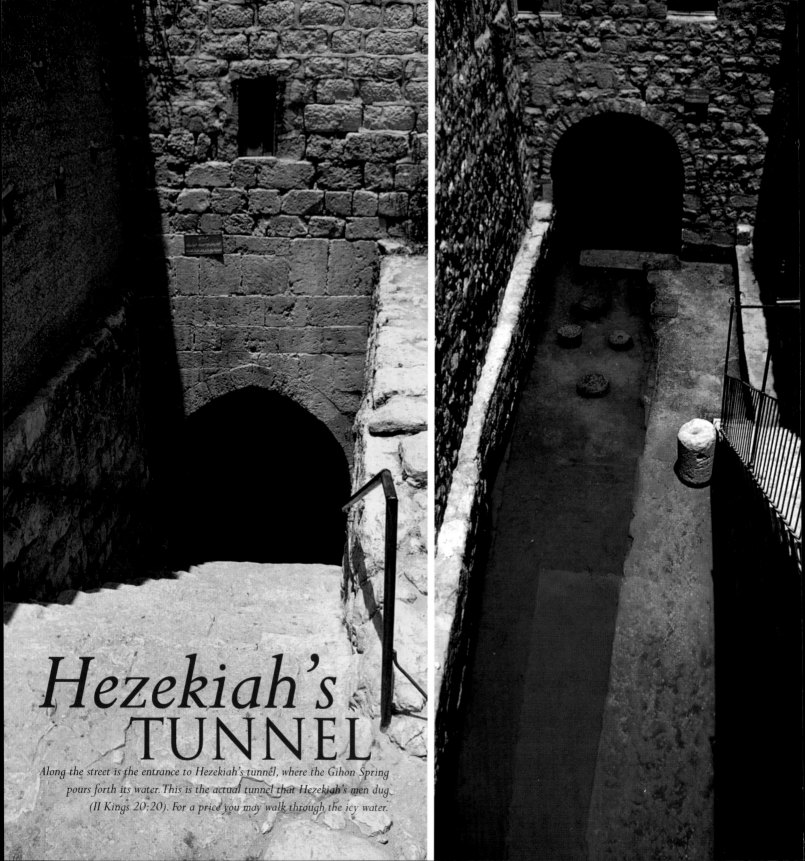

# Hezekiah's TUNNEL

*Along the street is the entrance to Hezekiah's tunnel, where the Gihon Spring pours forth its water. This is the actual tunnel that Hezekiah's men dug (II Kings 20:20). For a price you may walk through the icy water.*

OPPOSITE: *The water from Hezekiah's tunnel flows into the pool of Siloam, or Silwan, which was within the walls in ancient times. The Lord Jesus sent the man born blind to the pool of Siloam to wash, and he came seeing (John 9:6-7).*

ABOVE: *A major source of water for Jerusalem came from Solomon's pools some nine miles south (Eccles. 2:6). Herod the Great is actually the one who had them built.*

RIGHT: *It is easy to spot the offset join marks where the two teams of diggers met in the underground tunnel. It remains a remarkable engineering feat.*

ABOVE: *Note the rounded boulders of the lowest stones: they are the actual wall of the Jebusite city that David's men took (II Sam. 5:6-9).*

LEFT: *All over the hill of Ophel there are walls and walls. The upper walls are recent; the lower ones are ancient. Both Jotham and Manasseh built walls about Ophel (II Chron. 27:1-3; 33:13-14).*

# THE HILL *of Ophel*

OPPOSITE: *From the crest of the Mount of Offence, looking across the Kidron Valley, there is a clear view of the hill of Ophel as it stretches south from the temple area.*

ABOVE: *The rounded stones of Jebusite walls support the stepped stone building.*

BELOW: *The house of Ahiel (5) was built on the slope of the stepped stone structure at a later time and was destroyed in 586 B.C.*

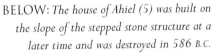

*The stepped stone structure (4) is built on older Jebusite walls. Archaeologists believe that it is a retaining wall for Solomon's palace, thirteen years in the building (I Kings 7:1). This is further proof that Scripture is correct. First Kings 9:15 claims that Solomon built the walls of Jerusalem, Hazor, Megiddo, and Gezer.*

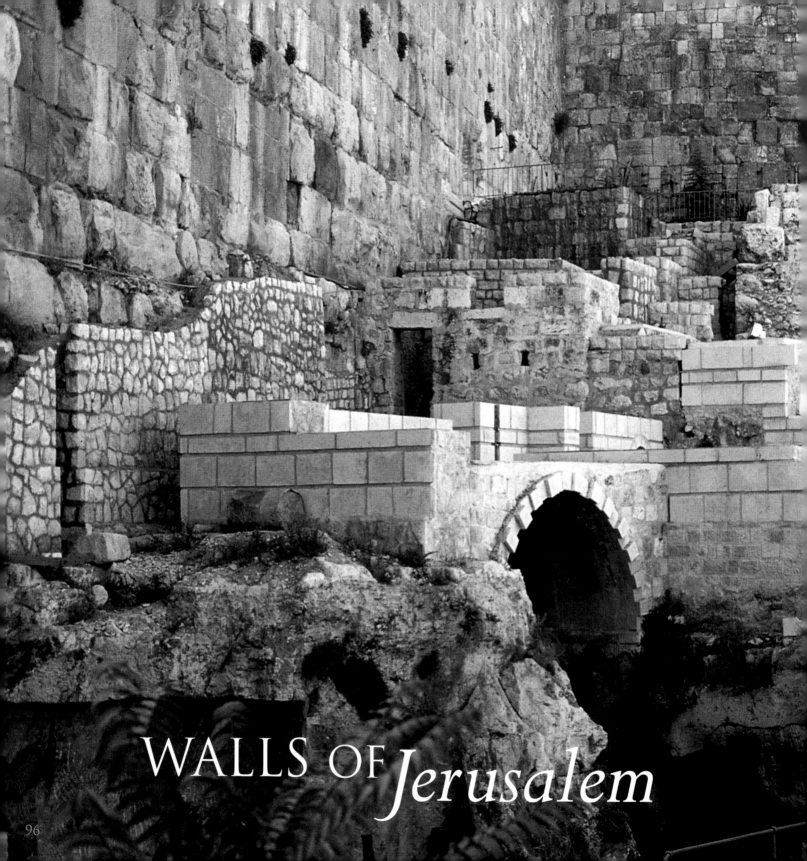

WALLS OF *Jerusalem*

LEFT: *The triple gate was a double gate in the first century.*

LEFT: *The Dung Gate has been widened to allow automotive traffic through it.*

LEFT: *Archaeologists have restored the grand staircase to the gates on the south side of the temple. The lower blocks on the wall are the huge Herodian stones; the upper, smaller stones are from Suleiman the Magnificent.*

LEFT: *There are many excavations along the present southern wall of the city.*

The Church of St. Peter Gallicantu (of the cock crowing) is a traditional church b[uilt]
over the palace of Caiaphas. It commemorates Peter's denial (Matt. 26:69-75). Th[e]
area was within the walls in the first century but is now outsi[de]

RIGHT: *Looking from Gallicantu southward, you can see the traditional "Field of Blood" (Aceldama, Acts 1:18-19) in which Judas hanged himself over the cliff and fell to his death.*

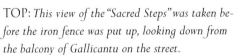

TOP: *This view of the "Sacred Steps" was taken before the iron fence was put up, looking down from the balcony of Gallicantu on the street.*

LEFT: *The important thing about the church is the finding of the city street alongside it. We know that the streets were often stairs (Neh. 12:37). This is probably the very street up which the Lord Jesus was led to the palace of Caiaphas (John 18:24-28).*

# THE
# SACRED
# STEPS

ABOVE: *Just to the south of the Zion Gate is the traditional tomb of David. The cenotaph is empty; no one knows the location of the real tomb although it was known in New Testament times (Acts 2:29).*

# *South* from *the* ZION GATE

ABOVE: *Above the tomb of David is the Cenacle, the traditional site of the Last Supper (Luke 22:11-12). There is no question that the lower stonework is very ancient. Although the site cannot be proved, it is most probably the corner of the great Church of Zion that replaced the original Church of Zion, which was derived from the Church of the Upper Room (Acts 1:13-14).*

*The Zion Gate leads from Mount Zion south toward the Hinnom valley.*

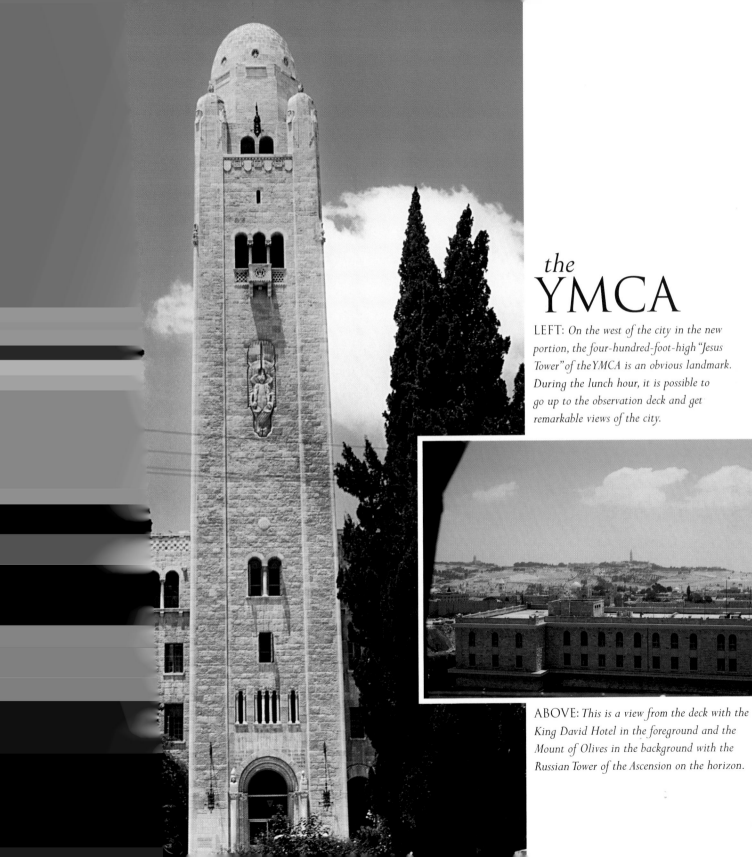

# the
# YMCA

LEFT: *On the west of the city in the new portion, the four-hundred-foot-high "Jesus Tower" of the YMCA is an obvious landmark. During the lunch hour, it is possible to go up to the observation deck and get remarkable views of the city.*

ABOVE: *This is a view from the deck with the King David Hotel in the foreground and the Mount of Olives in the background with the Russian Tower of the Ascension on the horizon.*

ABOVE: *The Citadel of David is built over part of the palace of Herod. The upper walls and the minaret are the work of Suleiman the Magnificent.*

RIGHT: *From the top of the old walls, looking westward, one can see the new Israeli Jerusalem in which a half million people now dwell. In the upper left of the scene is the Montefiore windmill, the first modern Jewish building outside the old walls (1860). That part of the new city is known as the Yemin Moshe Quarter.*

LEFT: *On the northeastern side is the Russian Orthodox Church of the Holy Trinity with its green domes. The Russian compound is on the site of the Assyrian camp in the siege against Jerusalem (II Kings 18:17).*

BELOW: *The Jaffa Gate is on the west side of the city near the Citadel of David. The Jaffa road led westward to the sea coast. The area is undergoing extensive excavations and traffic changes.*

# Knesset

BELOW: *Still farther west is the Hebrew University campus on which is a very unusual synagogue.*

BELOW: *In the Knesset gardens is [a] famous menorah, the seven-branched lamp stand, which was a gift from th[e] British Parliament in honor of Israeli independence.*

ABOVE: *Farther to the west in the new city is the Knesset, the Israeli Parliament.*

ABOVE: *Across the street from the Knesset is the Israel Museum. The Shrine of the Book is a special part of the museum in which the Dead Sea Scrolls are displayed. The white dome is modeled after the lid of the jars that contained the scrolls.*

ABOVE: *The museum displays horrifying pictures of the persecution.*

# Herzl Gardens & YAD VASHEM

RIGHT: *The best place to see a cedar of Lebanon in Israel is in the Herzl Gardens, a memorial to the founder of Zionism.*

*Nearby is Yad Vashem, the memorial to the Holocaust victims. The pillar is modeled after the smokestack of the ovens that consumed the bodies.*

*Inside is the eternal flame with the names of the death camps over the ashes of thirty thousand victims.*

*At the end of the display is a statue of Job.*

# MODEL of
# *Jerusalem*

RIGHT: *Alongside the temple was the Castle of Antonia with its four towers. The steps leading down were the ones that Paul was led up (Acts 21:35-40). In the foreground is the pool of Bethesda, with its five colonnades (the fifth one is across the center of the pool, John 5:2).*

RIGHT: *The model of the south wall of the temple complex faithfully shows the staircase (on the left) that led up to what is now called Robinson's arch. The two matched pairs of gates led up to the upper level.*

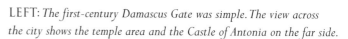

LEFT: *The first-century Damascus Gate was simple. The view across the city shows the temple area and the Castle of Antonia on the far side.*

In the courtyard of the Holyland Hotel is an archaeological model of
first-century Jerusalem. The model, which is a real help in perceiving
the structure of old Jerusalem, covers 75 by 150 feet, all to scale. This
is the reconstruction of Herod's temple, which faced east. Professor
Michael Avi-Yonah supervised every detail of the reconstruction.

# The DAMASCUS GATE &
## The Garden TOMB

RIGHT: *Coming back to the north wall of old Jerusalem, it is possible to get up on the wall in order to walk around the walls and look down.*

BELOW: *The Damascus Gate is the largest and most ornate of all the gates. The lower gate is really more important, dating from the first to second centuries of the Christian era.*

OPPOSITE RIGHT: *The cliff that is nearby is called Gordon's Calvary because "Chinese" Gordon, very devout believer, defended the authenticity of the site. The eye cavities are formed by cisterns that have been exposed.*

OPPOSITE LEFT: *Excavators have found a winepress, proving that it was a functioning garden*

A short distance from the Damascus Gate is the Garden Tomb. It is a lovely example of a first-century tomb. Although scholars argue over whether this or the Church of the Holy Sepulchre is the real location, the atmosphere at the Garden Tomb certainly appeals to the Protestant visitor.

ABOVE: *Solomon's rock quarries can be entered from the north wall.*

ABOVE: *For thousands of years people have cut white limestone from them to build Jerusalem.*

ABOVE: *The New Gate has no biblical significance. It is merely a modern, convenient way of getting into the Christian quarter.*

*The Herod Gate was so called because it was thought to lead to the palace of Herod Antipas. It is also called the Flower Gate because of the rosette above the gate.*

RIGHT: *The streets of old Jerusalem are too narrow to admit a moving van. When a family moves, they hire a porter to move their furniture. Here is a porter carrying a refrigerator on his back to a new location.*

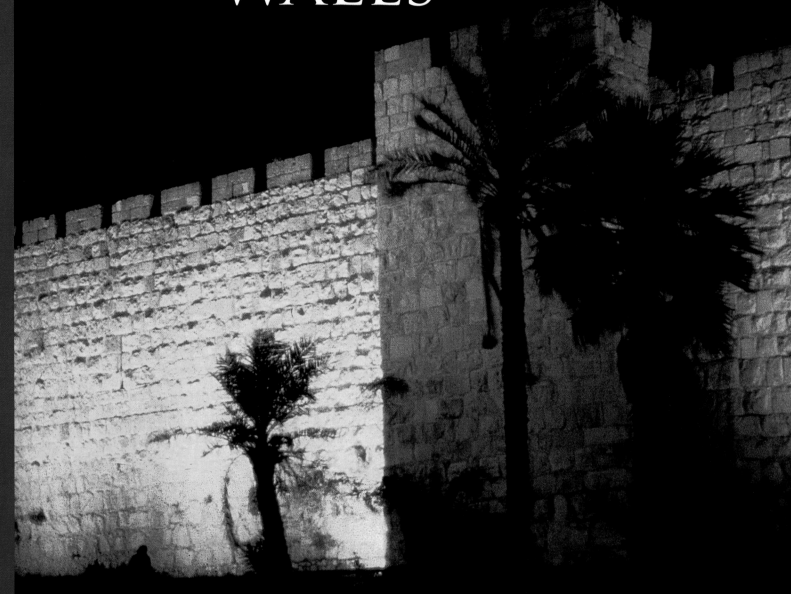

# WITHIN
# *Jerusalem's*
# WALLS

THE FIRST MENTION OF JERUSALEM IN SCRIPTURE CONCERNS ADONI-ZEDEC, KING OF JERUSALEM, GATHERING RESISTANCE AGAINST JOSHUA'S INVASION (JOSH. 10:1). IT IS UNIVERSALLY AGREED, HOWEVER, THAT MELCHIZEDEK, KING OF SALEM, RULED THE SAME CITY CENTURIES BEFORE (GEN. 14:18; HEB. 7:1-2). IT IS "THE HOLY CITY" BEYOND ALL OTHERS (REV. 11:2). IN THE FUTURE GOD HAS PROMISED TO CREATE A NEW JERUSALEM, HOLY JERUSALEM, AS AN ETERNAL ABODE FOR HIS PEOPLE (REV. 21:10). THERE ARE MANY DIFFERENT WAYS OF ORGANIZING WALKING TOURS OF THE OLD CITY. YOU CAN BEGIN FROM ANY GATE.

# [PART 6] WITHIN *Jerusalem's* WALLS

TOP: *The night walk around Jerusalem is especially enjoyable, although it was not to Nehemiah, because the walls were in ruins (Neh. 2:12-17). The walls are floodlit every night, but you will need a tripod for time photographs or a flash for close-ups.*

ABOVE: *Jerusalem presents a lovely panorama at night.*

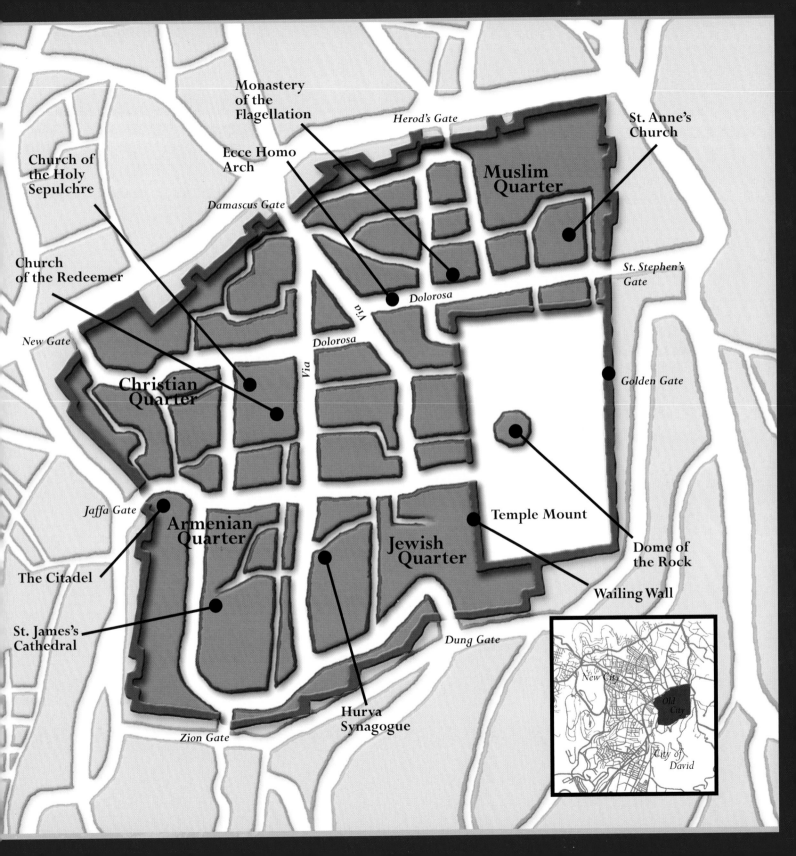

Monastery
of the
Flagellation

Herod's Gate

St. Anne's
Church

Ecce Homo
Arch

Muslim
Quarter

Church of
the Holy
Sepulchre

Damascus Gate

Church
of the Redeemer

St. Stephen's
Gate

Via
Dolorosa

Dolorosa

New Gate

Via

Christian
Quarter

Golden Gate

Temple Mount

Jaffa Gate

Armenian
Quarter

Jewish
Quarter

The Citadel

Dome of
the Rock

St. James's
Cathedral

Wailing Wall

Dung Gate

Hurva
Synagogue

Zion Gate

New City

Old
City

City of
David

LEFT: *Inside the Citadel of David the audience sits on folding chairs watching the history of Jerusalem unfold as the different time periods are illuminated by the architecture of the citadel. The program goes through the Jewish, Roman, Arab, Crusader, and Turkish periods.*

LEFT: *After the program, the streets of the city are deserted. King David Street is normally packed with people. Depending on the situation, the authorities may discourage walking at night.*

# *Jerusalem* AT NIGHT

*The Jaffa Gate area is a good place to begin because the sound and light program, "A Stone in David's Tower," is put on in English several nights in the week at the Citadel of David.*

*The western wall of the temple is always floodlit. Jews pray there at all hours of the day and night.*

LEFT: *St. Stephen's Gate is illuminated with lights that give it a blue cast. It is called by his name because it is the closest gate to the place where he was stoned (Acts 7:55-60).*

LEFT: *During Ramadan the Damascus Gate is decorated with lights and thousands of people eat around the gate. Muslims fast during the daylight hours of Ramadan.*

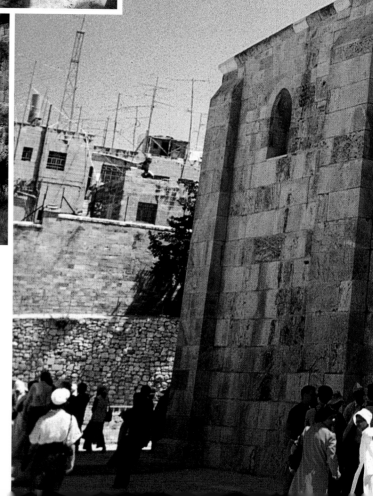

LEFT: *At St. Anne's is the excavation of the pool of Bethesda, with its five colonnades. One set of pillars went straight through the pool. The pool is seventy feet below ground level. This was the place in which the Lord healed the impotent man (John 5:2-9). A fifth-century church was built right over part of the pool.*

*Just inside St. Stephen's Gate is the Church of St. Anne, the finest example of Crusader architecture in Jerusalem. Any hymn sung in it sounds like a three-hundred-voice choir singing. St. Anne was the mother of Mary, according to tradition.*

RIGHT: *For daylight walks St. Stephen's Gate is a fine place to begin. It is easy for a bus to drop off tourists at the gate and pick them up later at another gate.*

# NEAR
## *St. Stephen's* GATE

BEHOLD
THE MAN!
[JOHN 19:5]

ABOVE: *The Via Dolorosa is the "way of sorrows" that the Lord Jesus walked on the way to the cross. The Ecce Homo Arch can be seen down the street. It is the traditional place from which Pilate displayed the Lord to the people (John 19:5).*

RIGHT: *The Chapel of the Flagellation commemorates the scourging of the Lord (John 19:1).*

# VIA *Dolorosa* &*the* CHURCH OF THE *Redeemer*

LEFT: *Near the Church of the Holy Sepulchre is the Lutheran Church of the Redeemer. It stands over the ruins of the Church of St. Mary Latin, a Crusader church.*

BELOW: *About twelve feet below the present street level is the Gabbatha, the pavement of Pilate's judgment hall (John 19:13). The Sisters of Zion convent is over the area now. It is still being debated as to whether the pavement is actually Pilate's or that of the second century laid on top of the old pavement.*

# CHURCH
## OF THE
# *Holy*
# *Sepulchre*

LEFT: *The view from the rooftop of the Church of the Holy Sepulchre, looking toward the Lutheran Church of the Redeemer.*

BELOW: *Alongside the church is the Russian Orthodox Chapel of St. Alexander. In the basement is a wall with great Roman stones, but "old" stones are lying upon "new" stones, proving that it is Hadrian's wall of the second century. The question of where the first-century wall ran is still open.*

ABOVE: *In reality David had nothing to do with the citadel; it was built by Herod the Great. The Phasael tower (on the left) Herod named after his brother. It was built on the foundations of a Hasmonean fort (note the bottom two courses of stone that jut out), and Suleiman built the walls higher with smaller stones in A.D. 1541. It was in this citadel that the son of Herod the Great, Herod Antipas, heard the trial of Christ (Luke 23:6-12).*

# CITADEL OF *David*

RIGHT: *This closer view of the tower shows that Herod's stones have carefully carved margins around the face of the stones.*

ABOVE: *From the tower one can also look down on the foundations of the Hasmonean walls that curve across the courtyard. They are older and more important than the present walls of the citadel, which were built by Crusaders and by Suleiman.*

TOP: *From the top of the tower there is a grand view over the walls to the new city beyond.* ABOVE: *There is also a fine view of the Christian quarter from the black dome of the Church of the Holy Sepulchre to the spire of the Church of St. Savior in the northwest corner.*

ABOVE: *This is a view over the Armenian quarter toward the Cathedral of St. James.*

LEFT: *There is a short walk through the Christian quarter to King David Street and the Jaffa Gate. This old view of the gate shows the proximity of the Citadel of David.*

ABOVE: *This is a view from the south walls looking toward the Mount of Olives.*

LEFT: *There are stairs down from the walls at the Zion Gate.*

# on TOP OF THE WALLS

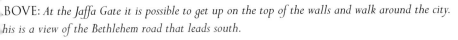

BOVE: *At the Jaffa Gate it is possible to get up on the top of the walls and walk around the city. his is a view of the Bethlehem road that leads south.*

# the Jewish QUARTER

RIGHT: *Archaeologists have uncovered Hezekiah's broad wall (twenty-three feet thick), which proves beyond doubt that Jerusalem included Mount Zion as well as Mount Moriah. This also confirms the scriptural portrait of Hezekiah's building efforts (II Chron. 32:2-5).*

*In the Jewish quarter is the Hurva Synagogue.*
*The memorial arch commemorates its destruction*
*by the Muslims.*

ABOVE: *The arches of some of the small shops have*
*been uncovered as well. They are about twenty-five feet*
*below the present ground level.*

LEFT: *Archaeologists have also found the Cardo, the*
*main north-south street in Roman Jerusalem. It had a*
*covered colonnade with shops lining the street.*

ABOVE: *Wilson's arch is part of a causeway that led from the temple area to Herod's palace on the western side of the city. It is the largest arch span found in Israel—over thirty feet. The area is now a place of prayer.*

LEFT: *The gate closest to the temple area is the Dung Gate, seen here from the inside. It is a natural entrance for those visiting the temple. It has been widened to admit buses.*

BELOW: *All that is left of Robinson's arch is the emplacement in the wall. It was a stairway that led from street level to the upper level of the temple.*

The Jews flock to the western wall of the temple area. It is their most holy site. They will not go up to the upper level, where the gold Dome of the Rock is, lest they should accidentally tread on the most holy place of the temple. The arch at the corner of the western wall and the old Turkish courthouse on the left lead to Wilson's arch.

RIGHT: *It is interesting to see the hyssop (caper berry,* Capparis sicula) *growing out of the wall (I Kings 4:33; Ps. 51:7).*

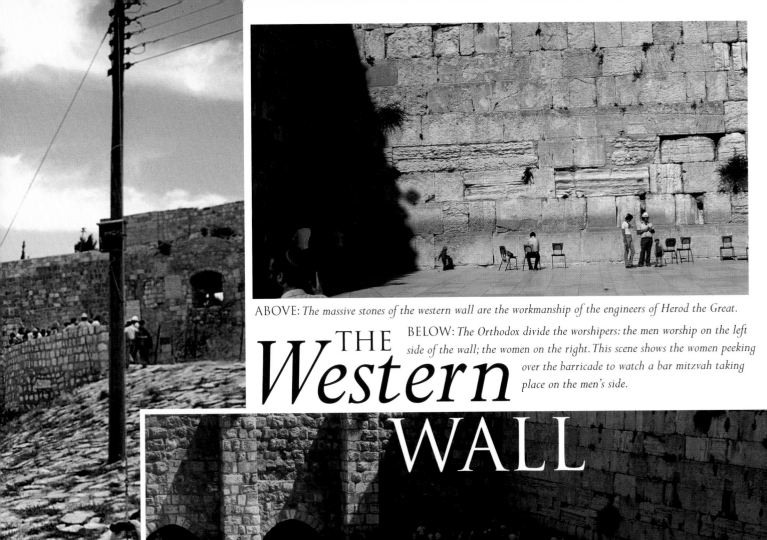

ABOVE: *The massive stones of the western wall are the workmanship of the engineers of Herod the Great.*

BELOW: *The Orthodox divide the worshipers: the men worship on the left side of the wall; the women on the right. This scene shows the women peeking over the barricade to watch a bar mitzvah taking place on the men's side.*

# THE *Western* WALL

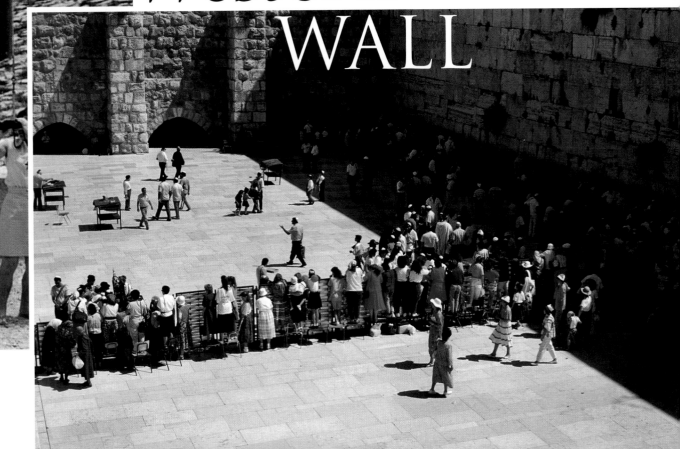

# THE *Dome* of the ROCK

RIGHT: *The Dome of the Rock is the third holiest place in the Muslim world (after Mecca and Medina). The faithful make pilgrimages to it just as they would to the other shrines.*

BELOW: *As you approach the Dome of the Rock, you must pass by the fountain (the Cup) at which the Muslims will stop to wash their face, hands, and feet before worshiping at the shrines.*

ABOVE: *The interior of the Dome of the Rock is adorned with marble pillars, gold, stained glass windows, and Persian carpets.*

LEFT: *The Dome of the Rock stands over the traditional place on which Abraham offered up his son Isaac to God (Gen. 22:1-12). Solomon built his temple on that site (I Kings 6:1ff.). Abd el-Malik built the dome in A.D. 691, which makes it the earliest existing example of Islamic architecture.*

LEFT: *The entrance to the Dome of the Rock is impressive. The tiling is magnificent.*

ABOVE: *Alongside the Dome of the Rock is the Dome of the Chain.*

RIGHT: *The Mosque of El Aksa (the edge) is built on the southern edge of the temple area. It used to have a silver dome on it; now it also has a black dome.*

# THE *Temple* MOUNT

o the northwest of the Dome of the Rock is the Dome of the Spirits. Some think that this is the original location of the most holy place in the *emple. The little dome frames the Russian Tower of the Ascension on the crest of the Mount of Olives. Between them, on a lower level out of sight, *s the Golden Gate. This is one of the interesting alignments in the area.*

ABOVE: *A view of the walled-up Golden Gate from the temple area. The Tower of the Ascension crowns the Mount of Olives.*

RIGHT: *Turning one's back on the Golden Gate and looking toward the Dome of the Spirits, it is striking to see the dome of the Church of the Holy Sepulchre in that same alignment!*

# from
# *Jerusalem*
# TO MASADA

THE JERICHO ROAD RUNS THROUGH A
DESOLATE PORTION OF LAND STRETCH-
ING FROM JERUSALEM TO THE DEAD
SEA, THE LOWEST POINT ON EARTH.
THE FAMOUS DEAD SEA SCROLLS WERE
FOUND NEARBY, AND MASADA, ONCE A
MAGNIFICENT PALACE AND THE LAST
STRONGHOLD OF THE JEWS AGAINST
THE ROMANS, IS JUST A SHORT DRIVE
FROM THE SHORES OF THE DEAD SEA.

# from Jerusalem [PART 7] TO MASADA

RIGHT: *In the southern part of the Dead Sea you can see "saltbergs" floating.*

ABOVE: *An irritable camel will tell you that he does not want you getting on him.*

Mediterranean
Sea

Sea of
Galilee

Jordan

Jerusalem

Dead Sea

Jerusalem

Wadi Qelt

Jericho

Mar Saba

Qumran

**Dead
Sea**

En Gedi

Masada

# THE CHURCH of
## *Mary, Martha,* & LAZARUS

RIGHT: *The interior of the church has illustrations of biblical events.*

BELOW: *Nearby is the traditional tomb of Lazarus. Whether it is the actual tomb is impossible to verify, but it is an example of a first-century tomb in the area. The burial chamber was twenty-five feet below the ground. When the Lord Jesus commanded, "Lazarus, come forth," Lazarus was propelled up the stairs and stood before Him, "bound hand and foot with graveclothes" (John 11:44).*

*The Church of Mary, Martha, and Lazarus commemorates this dearly loved family.*

TEMPLVM
SANCTO
LAZARO
DICATVM

145

# THE *Jericho* ROAD

The Jericho Road is a desolate portion of land. It is easy to see how bandits could hide along the way to rob solitary travelers (Luke 10:30). As the crow flies, it is only fifteen miles from Jerusalem to the Jordan, but by the switchbacks it is much longer.

SEA LEVEL

LEFT: The Jericho Road descends eastward from Jerusalem (twenty-five hundred feet above sea level), over the Mount of Olives (twenty-seven hundred feet above sea level), to the Dead Sea (thirteen hundred feet below sea level). It is a surprise to get to the sea-level sign and realize that from that point on you are below the level of the ocean.

BELOW: *There are Bedouin encampments along the road. The tents provide much-needed shade, but the temperature is still horrible.*

BOTTOM: *There is a traditional "Good Samaritan Inn" along the way.*

*A camel comes up from a drink at Elisha's spring (II Kings 2:19-22). It is still the water source for Jericho.*

# Jericho

TOP: *Jericho has always been known as the city of palm trees (Deut. 34:3; II Chron. 28:15). It is famous today for the delicious "Jericho dates."*

RIGHT: *It is also famous for the great sycamore trees. They usually have several trunks coming from a single root, which makes them easy to climb, as Zacchaeus demonstrated (Luke 19:1-10).*

TOP: *The old city of Jericho is one great heap of excavations and piles of dirt all over the tel.*

LEFT: *Everywhere you look there are excavations of city walls from many different periods in the history of Jericho.*

ABOVE: *Archaeologists believe that this round tower is part of the oldest city wall that has been discovered any place in the world. It goes back a great deal before the time of Joshua (Josh. 6). The Holy Land is a land bridge between Europe, Asia, and Africa. From earliest times the cities had to be defended.*

# THE MOUNT of *Temptation*

The mountain ridge overlooking Jericho is called the Mount of Temptation because of its traditional identification with the temptation of the Lord Jesus (Matt. 4:1). There are monasteries clinging to the cliff.

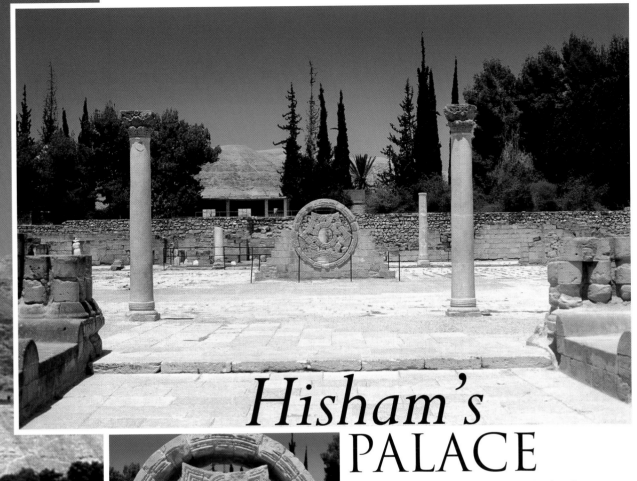

# Hisham's PALACE

ABOVE: *Near the tel of Jericho is Hisham's palace, built in A.D. 724. It was a winter resort for khalifs of the Omayyad dynasty.*

LEFT: *A close-up of a window from the palace.*

LEFT: *A mosaic floor from the palace depicts the tree of life.*

RIGHT: *The rugged hills around Qumran are honeycombed with caves.*

BELOW: *There are a number of cisterns to try to trap every drop of rainwater that might fall.*

RIGHT: *Cave 4 is an obvious sight from Qumran. It is the famous place in which were found about forty thousand fragments of ancient manuscripts. Every book of the Old Testament except Esther has been identified, along with a number of extrabiblical works, some previously unknown.*

# Qumran

*Farther south along the Dead Sea is Qumran, a monastic community of the first century. These people copied and preserved the Scriptures and other religious documents.*

RIGHT: *There is a large meeting and dining room in the monastery.*

RIGHT: *Archaeologists have identified the scriptorium where the Dead Sea Scrolls were copied.*

# Qumran

RIGHT: *There are baths for ritual immersion.*

BELOW: *The remains of the watchtower still guard the monastery. It is a good place from which to view the complex of buildings.*

# WADI QELT

The Monastery of St. George is about seventeen miles from Jerusalem in the Wadi Qelt that stretches toward the Dead Sea. From the road it is a twenty-minute hike down the canyon to the monastery in 100° temperature in summer.

BELOW INSET: *St. George dates from about* A.D. *480. A similar monastery is Mar Saba, built in* A.D. *482 in the Kidron Valley. Women must wait in a tower outside while men only visit Mar Saba. Not even a female sheep is allowed in!*

155

En Gedi (the spring of the goat) is now a nature reserve. It was one of David's hiding places from the pursuit of Saul (I Sam. 24).

RIGHT: *The Nubian ibex is a large mountain goat that can be seen high up on the cliffs. The ibex has been reintroduced to the wild and is doing well. The word ibex is translated "antelope" or "wild ox" (Deut. 14:5). This example is from the Biblical Zoo in Jerusalem, which has been expanded and is now called the Tisch Family Zoological Gardens.*

# EN GEDI

TOP: *This is sunrise (5 A.M.), seen from En Gedi, looking across the Dead Sea toward the eastern hills.*

ABOVE: *It is a beautiful experience to hike the nature trails at the En Gedi reserve.*

RIGHT: *There are date palms loaded with dates.*

157

ABOVE: *There are many excavations in the En Gedi area.*

BELOW: *One of the major discoveries is a synagogue at En Gedi. Curiously, there is a swastika on the floor of the synagogue. That was an ancient symbol, no connection with the Nazi variety.*

# EN GEDI

*There are public beaches at En Gedi for swimming in the oily, salt-filled water.*

RIGHT: *It is not possible to swim normally in the Dead Sea; swimmers bob like a cork on the surface of the water. They will often "ham it up," reading books or newspapers while they bob. Ocean water is 3 percent salt; the Dead Sea is about 30 percent salt. The Dead Sea is shrinking every year from evaporation.*

BELOW: *Now it is possible to ride cable cars from the Dead Sea level up to the top of Masada.*

BELOW: *The alternative to the cable cars is the snake trail that zigzags up the eastern face of the rock. It is a two-hour hike in incredible heat.*

LEFT: *From the top of Masada you can see the Roman forts and the wall of circumvallation built to keep the defenders from fleeing.*

# MASADA

*Masada as seen from the Judean hills. The stair steps on the left lead to the winter palace of Herod the Great; the Roman rampart is on the right. It took the Romans three years to build the rampart up to a level that they could storm the walls of the fortress (A.D. 67-70). This may be the stronghold (metsudah) that David and his men fled to (I Sam. 24:22).*

*The wall paintings are now protected by glass.*

LEFT: *There are mosaic floors in the palace on the upper level.*

# *Herod's* PALACE

TOP: *On the northern tip of Masada is Herod's palace in three levels. Some of the pillars and wall paintings are still in place.*

LEFT: *The view from Masada looking south toward the Dead Sea.*

BELOW: *There are huge cisterns to collect any drop of rainwater that might fall. When it did not rain, slaves carried the water up from the base thirteen hundred feet below.*

BOTTOM: *The oldest-known synagogue in the world is on the top of Masada.*

ABOVE: *Many of the missiles that the Romans catapulted on the defenders are still to be seen.*

# MASADA

There are large storerooms on the top level of Masada

# *from* Jerusalem TO EILAT

SOUTH OF BETHLEHEM IS HEBRON
AND NEARBY MAMRE, BOTH IM-
PORTANT TO ABRAHAM. GOING
FARTHER SOUTH, YOU TRAVEL
THROUGH ANOTHER ABRAHAMIC
SITE, BEERSHEBA, TO THE NEGEV
DESERT AND ON TO TIMNA,
KNOWN FOR ITS COPPER MINES.

# *from* [PART 8]
## *Jerusalem*
# TO EILAT

TOP: *The manger square is surrounded by churches, mosques, and shops.*

ABOVE: *Down the coast of the Sinai Peninsula some eight miles lies the Coral Island (or Pharaoh's Island). There are ruins of a Crusader fort on it.*

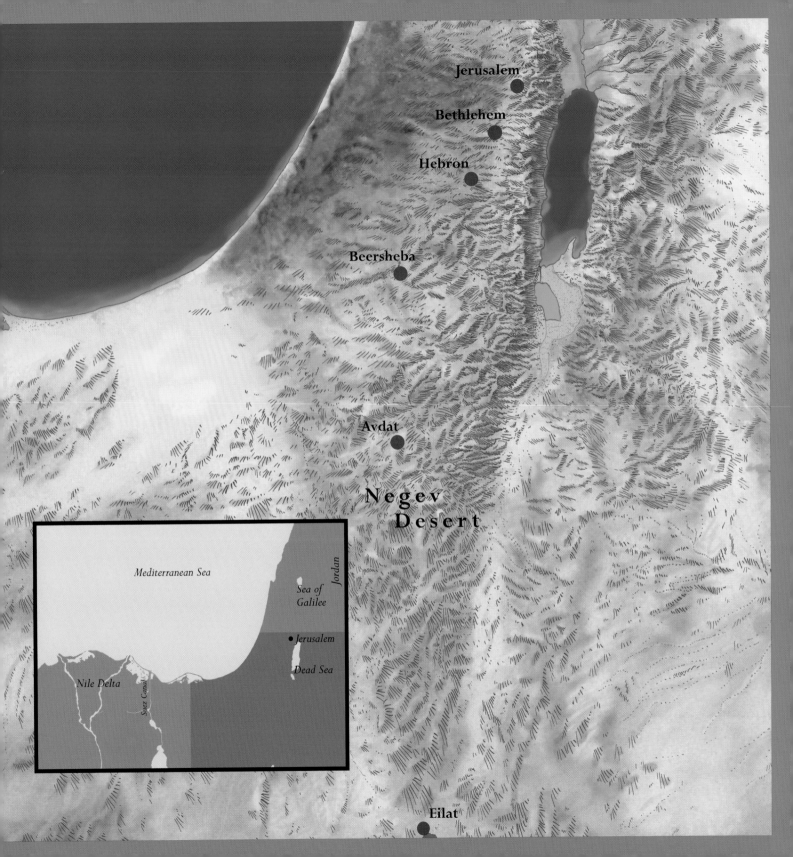

Jerusalem

Bethlehem

Hebron

Beersheba

Avdat

Negev
Desert

Eilat

Mediterranean Sea

Jordan

Sea of
Galilee

Jerusalem

Dead Sea

Nile Delta

Suez Canal

# CHURCH *of*THE *Nativity*

RIGHT: *Outside the church are statues of Jerome, who translated the Latin Vulgate in Bethlehem, and, of course, of Mary.*

RIGHT: *The ringing of the bell tower has been used to mark the hour over Israeli radio.*

BELOW: *The door to the church is so low that everyone must bow to enter. That is not an accident. When the Muslims invaded the land, their habit was to ride their horses into churches and stable them there. The monks at Bethlehem determined that their door would be so low that no horse could get in, and any person would bow in reverence! They call it "the door of humility."*

The massive Church of the Nativity dominates the scene. It was built by the emperor Constantine the Great in A.D. 312, making it the oldest continuously used church in the world.

ABOVE: *On a lower level under the altar is the alleged place of the birth of the Lord, marked with a silver star set in a marble floor. There is no way to prove that this is the actual place, but it has to be within a stone's throw in as small a place as Bethlehem.*

RIGHT: *Nearby is a stone manger, which is declared to be the place where the Lord lay.*

ABOVE: *The interior of the church looks very old. There is a trap door in the floor to show the original mosaic floor.*

LEFT: *The ancient floor as seen through the trap door.*

# INSIDE *the* CHURCH *of* THE *Nativity*

*The Shepherds' Fields are the best-authenticated place in the Holy Land. Bethlehem lies on the hill in the background. The fields stretch in one direction from the town. Somewhere around those fields the angel appeared to the shepherds, announcing the birth of the Savior, "Christ the Lord" (Luke 2:11).*

# AROUND
# *Bethlehem*

LEFT: *On the busiest main street of Bethlehem is the tomb of Rachel. She died giving birth to Benjamin and was buried in Bethlehem (Gen. 35:16-19). Jacob was buried with Leah in the cave of Machpelah (Gen. 50:13).*

BELOW: *Just a few miles from Bethlehem lies the Herodion, the man-made hill that was supposed to be the tomb of Herod the Great. There is no tomb there, and no one knows where Herod was actually buried.*

# HEBRON

The one magnificent sight in Hebron is the great shrine over the cave of Machpelah, built by Herod the Great. It is a place sacred to Jews, Muslims, and Christians. BELOW INSET: Abraham bought the cave to bury his wife, Sarah (Gen. 23:19). Abraham, Isaac, and Jacob were all buried in the cave of Machpelah (Gen. 25:9; 35:27-29; 50:13). The view shows the empty cenotaph of Abraham. The Muslims will allow no one to enter the cave in which the patriarchs were actually buried.

LEFT: *The huge stones in the wall by the entrance are definitely Herodian stones of the same type used in the temple construction.*

LEFT: *Hebron is ten miles south of Bethlehem. It is a drab and dusty town. David reigned in Hebron for seven and a half years (II Sam. 5:5). This picture, taken in 1969, shows how the Israelis beautified the town square by making a pool and planting trees and shrubs in front of the shrine of Machpelah.*

LEFT: *In more recent years the same view from the steps of the shrine shows how the trees have grown into an oasis of greenery. The rest of the town is still drab.*

ABOVE: *Close to Hebron are the excavations of Mamre, another place where Abraham lived (Gen. 18:1).*

# *Mamre* & BEERSHEBA

LEFT: *Many excavations are clearly marked.*

RIGHT: *The gate of Beersheba is easy to see.*

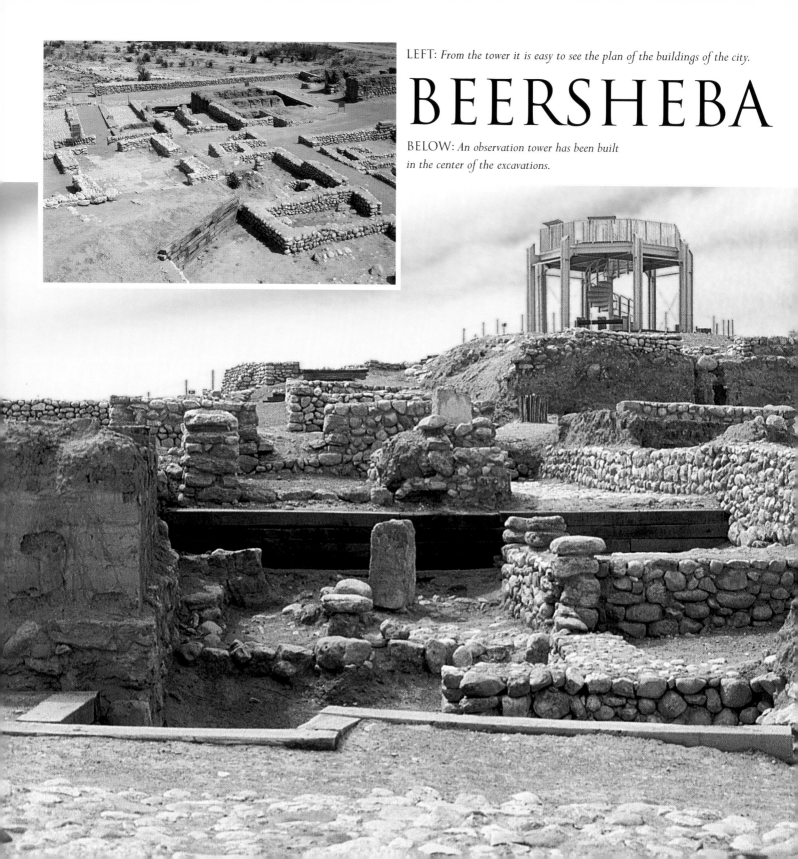

LEFT: *From the tower it is easy to see the plan of the buildings of the city.*

# BEERSHEBA

BELOW: *An observation tower has been built in the center of the excavations.*

ABOVE: *Beyond the excavations is the modern industrial city of Beersheba.*

RIGHT: *On Thursdays the Camel Market at Beersheba swarms with activity.*

LEFT: *On rare occasions you might see camels eating thorn bushes only a camel could swallow*

ABOVE: *From Beersheba south you are traveling in the hot Negev Desert. Once in a while you have to wait for a shepherd to get his flock off the road.*

# THE *Negev* DESERT

BELOW: *Sometimes you will see a flock of goats spread out on a hillside. What are they finding to eat?*

*Here and there is an acacia tree (shittah), all the leaves shed in the heat of summer. The ark of the covenant was made of shittim wood (the plural of shittah, Exod. 25:10-13).*

# AVDAT

RIGHT: *The spring at Avdat permits a little vegetation in the heat.*

BELOW: *The archaeological sign at Avdat.*

AVDAT

AN ANCIENT CARAVAN
STATION ON THE
MAIN ROUTE FROM
PETRA AND ELATH
TO THE MEDITERRANEAN,
ESTABLISHED BY THE
NABATEANS IN THE
3rd CENTURY B.C.
THE CITY FLOURISHED
IN THE ROMAN PERIOD
(3rd-4th CENTURY A.D.)
AND BYZANTINE PERIOD
(5th-7th CENTURY A.D.)
AND FELL INTO DECLINE
SHORTLY AFTER THE
ARAB CONQUEST.

RIGHT: *The excavations on the top of Avdat have uncovered a winepress. A Byzantine church has also been found.*

*Some thirty-nine miles south of Beersheba is Avdat, a caravan stop with a large spring of water. The view from the top of the mesa is desert, shimmering in the heat, as far as the eye can see.*

# TIMNA

RIGHT: *Solomon had nothing to do with the Pillars of Solomon, but they are impressive enough to deserve some important man's name!*

ABOVE: *Near Timna is the mighty rock formation called the Pillars of Solomon.*

LEFT: *Timna is about ninety-five miles south of Avdat, a place of copper mines and rugged rocks. This rock formation is called the Lion of Timna.*

There are few regions on the face of the earth that are as barren, desolate, and hot as the Sinai Peninsula along the shores of the Red Sea.

BELOW INSET: *Sunrise over the Saudi Arabian mountains at 5 A.M. is the only moment it is cool along the Sinai Peninsula. The temperature has been recorded at 132° along the Red Sea.*

RIGHT: *There are resort hotels now along the shore of the Red Sea, complete with sandy beaches.*

BELOW RIGHT: *Traveling 110 miles south from Avdat brings you to Eilat on the shores of the Red Sea. It is the southernmost city in modern Israel. The Israelites passed by Eilat and Ezion Geber on the way to the Holy Land (Deut. 2:8). King Solomon built his fleet in Ezion Geber, which is near Eilat (I Kings 9:26). King Azariah (Uzziah) rebuilt Eilat and restored it to Judah (II Kings 14:22).*

# EILAT

ABOVE: *The original beaches had no sand; they were water-tumbled rocks. This view looks toward the city of Aqaba in Jordan.*

# THE
# RED SEA

OPPOSITE TOP LEFT: *In Eilat it is possible to get a ride in a glass-bottomed boat to see multitudes of fish.*

OPPOSITE TOP RIGHT: *The sergeant major with its stripes is a common sight.*

LEFT: *This is a large brain coral.*

BELOW: *The beautiful coral formations of the Red Sea.*

# from *Jerusalem* TO ASHKELON

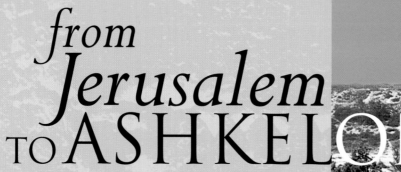

GOING WESTWARD FROM JERUSALEM,
YOU COME TO THE SHEPHELAH, THE
ROLLING HILL COUNTRY BETWEEN
THE CENTRAL MOUNTAINS AND THE
COASTAL PLAIN. THIS PIEDMONT RE-
GION WAS VITAL TO THE DEFENSE OF
JERUSALEM. IT WAS FOR CENTURIES A
BATTLEGROUND BETWEEN THE
PHILISTINES AND THE ISRAELITES.

# *from* [PART 9]
# *Jerusalem* TO ASHKELON

ABOVE: *David slew Goliath in the Valley of Elah. If you look closely at the stones in the valley, you will find every size and shape, but all smooothed by the tumbling action of the winter torrents.*

RIGHT: *A view from the national park at Ashkelon.*

PART 9

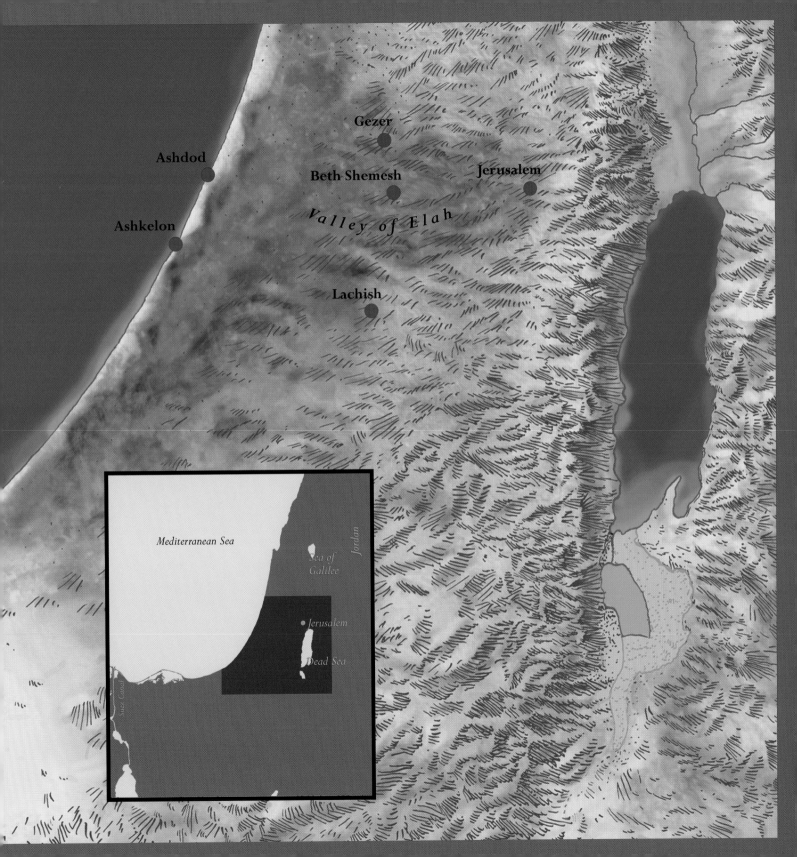

Gezer

Ashdod

Beth Shemesh

Jerusalem

Ashkelon

*Valley of Elah*

Lachish

*Mediterranean Sea*

*Jordan*

*Sea of Galilee*

• *Jerusalem*

*Dead Sea*

*Suez Canal*

The whole Shephelah region is honeycombed with caves and rock quarries. Unless you know the region, you may miss seeing them. Sometimes just walking around a hill will bring a cave to your attention. David escaped to the cave of Adullam (I Sam. 22:1), but which one that was is difficult to prove.

# Beth Shemesh
# &GEZER

BELOW: *Directly west from Jerusalem was Beth Shemesh (the house of the sun). When the Philistines wanted to get rid of the ark because of the plague, they put it on a cart, and two cows carried it to Beth Shemesh, where the Israelites received it with joy (I Sam. 6:11-13). It was on the northern border of Judah (Josh. 15:10). Amaziah and Jehoash fought at Beth Shemesh; Amaziah lost (II Kings 14:11-13). There have been many excavations at Beth Shemesh, but only a few walls are visible.*

RIGHT: *Northwards from Beth Shemesh is Gezer, seen here on the crest of the hill. Not much can be seen there because the high place with the standing stones has been reburied to protect the site. Gezer was conquered by Pharaoh and given as a present to Solomon, who fortified it with the Solomonic gate and walls as he did other fortress cities (I Kings 9:15-17).*

ABOVE: *Some caves turn out to be huge. Many times they will have marks of quarrying. This one has white limestone. A hymn sung in the cave will reverberate as in a cathedral.*

Traveling south from Beth Shemesh, you will come to a deserted valley. The bus stops and everyone gets out, but there are no ruins to see. This is the valley of Elah, and as you look toward the east, you see the hill on which Saul and the Israelites stood when they faced the Philistines (I Sam. 17:1-4).

# Valley of ELAH

TOP: *Toward the west, the Mediterranean side, is the hill on which Goliath stalked, hurling curses and defiance at the Israelites (I Sam. 17:10-43).*

ABOVE: *In the valley floor was the brook, now a dry streambed, with multitudes of water-tumbled stones. As David passed across the streambed, he stopped to pick up five smooth stones (I Sam. 17:40).*

RIGHT: *Excavations show how intricate the defenses of the city were.*

RIGHT: *Archaeologists have uncovered the foundations of a double gate system as well.*

# LACHISH

RIGHT: *In the center of the city was a massive governor's palace.*

Further down the coast is another Philistine city, Ashkelon. Samson slew thirty Philistines in Ashkelon (Judg. 14:19). The lord of Ashkelon sent an offering when the ark was returned to Israel (1 Sam. 6:16-17). The prophets pronounced judgment against Ashkelon (Jer. 25:17-20; Amos 1:8). Today Ashkelon has mostly deserted beaches with beautiful white sand.

LEFT: On the Sabbath, however, the same view looks more like Coney Island.

RIGHT: Traveling all the way to the
coast, you can find the Philistine city
Ashdod. When the Philistines captured the
ark, they took it to Ashdod, but they soon
found that the plague came with it
(1 Sam. 5:1-7). King Uzziah warred
against the Philistines and broke down the
wall of Ashdod (II Chron. 26:6).

BELOW RIGHT: The Israelis have built
a breakwater to enable them to use Ashdod
as a harbor.

# *Ashdod*&
# ASHKELON

ABOVE: *There is a place in the desert near Gaza that is called Philip's Fountain. It is an attempt to identify the place where Philip baptized the Ethiopian eunuch (Acts 8:38).*

203

Ashkelon is now a national park.
The ancient wall surrounds many
excavated ruins.

LEFT: There are extensive
excavations in the Ashkelon
park that travelers may
walk through.

ABOVE: *The Council Chamber at Ashkelon
is another large area.*

RIGHT: *This is a statue of the
goddess Isis, with Horus.*

204

# ASHKELON

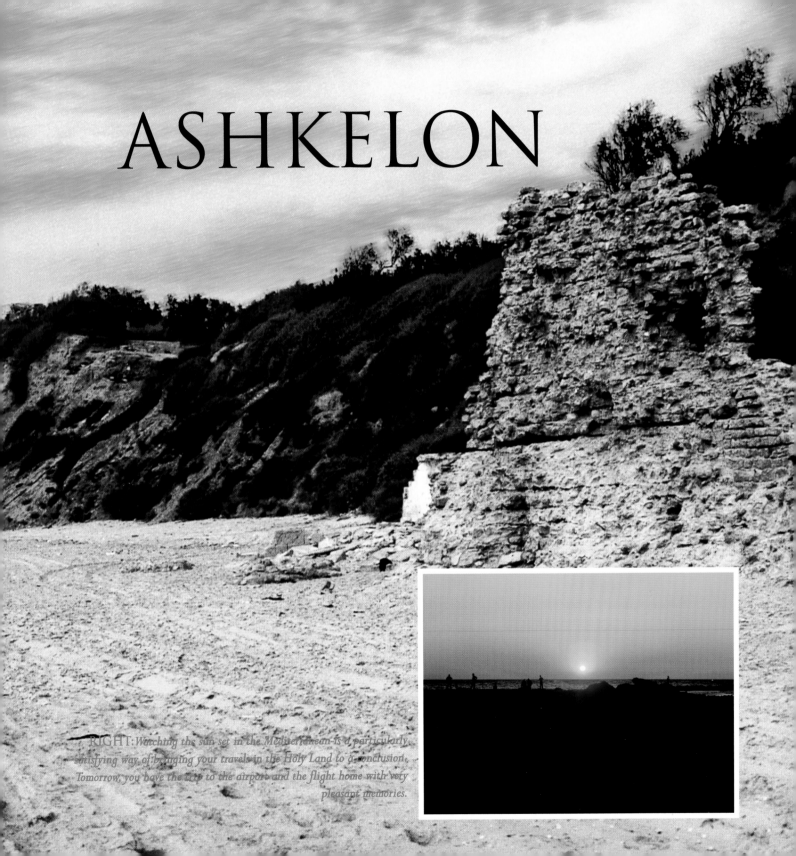

RIGHT: *Watching the sun set in the Mediterranean is a particularly satisfying way of bringing your travels in the Holy Land to a conclusion. Tomorrow, you have the trip to the airport and the flight home with very pleasant memories.*

# TO *Jordan* &OTHER LANDS

CROSSING OVER TO THE EAST BANK OF

THE JORDAN RIVER BRINGS ONE TO THE

HASHEMITE KINGDOM OF JORDAN. A

MORE TYPICAL WAY TO ARRIVE IS TO FLY

INTO THE CAPITAL OF AMMAN.

# PART 10

# TO *Jordan* & OTHER LANDS

BELOW: *The Pyramids still brood over the land of Egypt as they did in the days of Joseph and Moses, but they looked more beautiful in those days, when there was brilliant white facing stone on them.*

ABOVE: *The main streets of Jerash are lined with columns from one end to the other. This is the main north-south street, the principal business district of the city.*

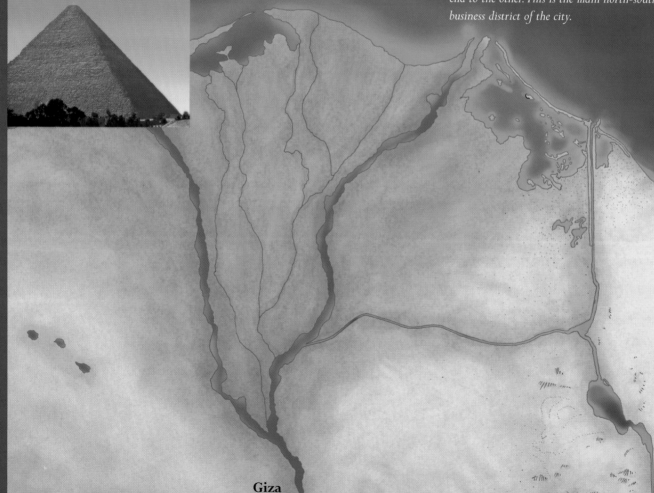

Giza

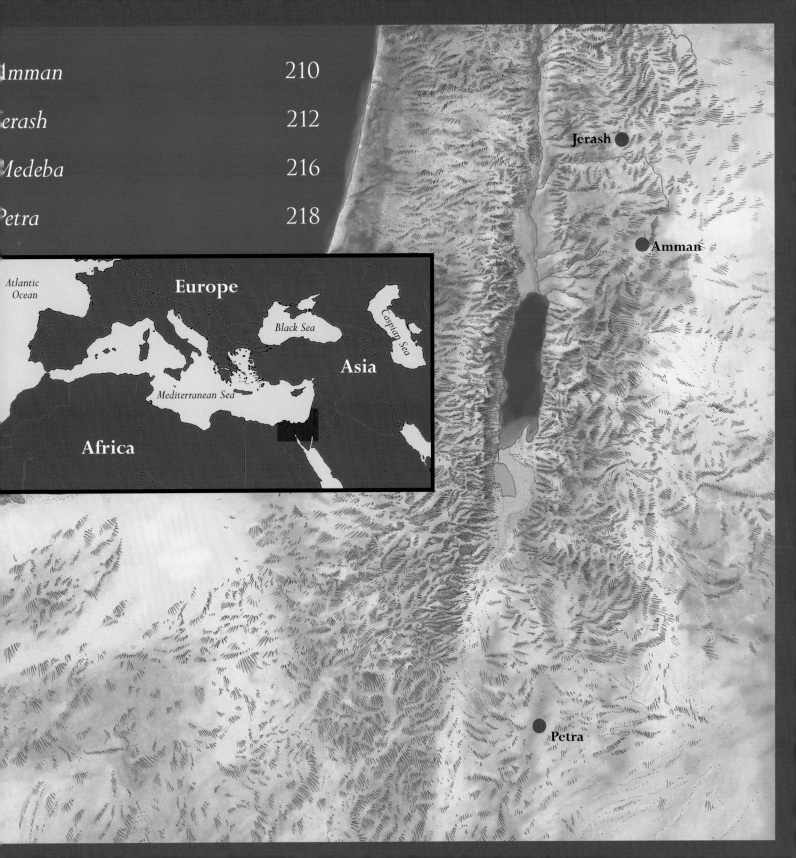

Atlantic
Ocean

Europe

Black Sea

Caspian Sea

Asia

Mediterranean Sea

Africa

# AMMAN

ABOVE: *Amman is the Rabbath-Ammon mentioned in the Old Testament. King Og's bed was there (Deut. 3:11). The city marked the border of Gad (Josh. 13:25). Joab besieged the city while David stayed at Jerusalem (II Sam. 11:1). Ezekiel prophesied that God would make it a stable for camels (Ezek. 25:5). This view, taken from the top of the old tel, shows the modern city of Amman surrounding it.*

RIGHT: *In Roman times the city was known as Philadelphia. The ruins of the Roman theater are near the tel.*

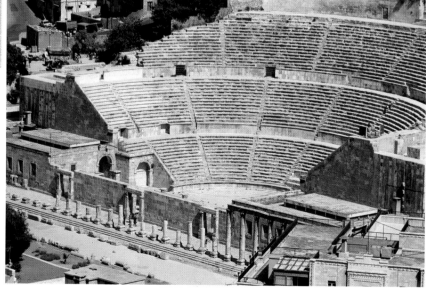

ABOVE: *The royal palace complex is impressive.*

LEFT: *A very distinctive mosque overlooking the area.*

ABOVE: *Outside the city, camels are a common sight (Gen. 24:63).*

BELOW: *Other ruins from the Roman period are in the area.*

211

# JERASH

ABOVE: *Jacob wrestled with the angel at the brook Jabbok and found his peace in submission (Gen. 32:22-30). The rectangular stones in the streambed are fish traps.*

RIGHT: *Jerash (or Gerasa) was one of the ten important cities in the Decapolis region, where the Lord Jesus ministered (Mark 5:20; 7:31). It is recognized today as the best example of a Roman city excavated in the Holy Land. Colonnaded streets ran the length and breadth of the city.*

The ruins of the temple of Zeus overlook the forum as the temple of Zeus (Jupiter) did at Lystra (Acts 14:13)

BELOW: *The color of the columns shows which sections were long buried and which were put back into place.*

BOTTOM: *A colonnaded Roman forum is near the theater.*

RIGHT: *The ruins of the south Roman theater in Jerash are well preserved. The theater was estimated to seat about five thousand.*

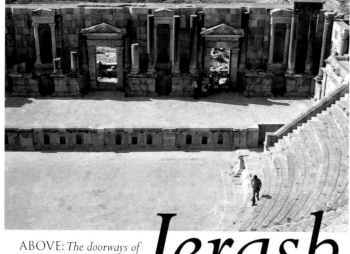

ABOVE: *The doorways of the stage are still in place.*

# Jerash

RIGHT: *The stairs to the temple are an impressive approach.*

OPPOSITE: *In the center of the city the temple of Artemis dominated the view. She was the patron goddess of the city (as she was in Ephesus, Acts 19:28). The pillars stand fifty-four feet high.*

OPPOSITE INSET: *Traveling southward from Amman, you come to Medeba, an ancient Moabite to[wn]. It is mentioned several times in Scripture (Num 21:30; Josh. 13:9[,] 16). It is close to Mount Nebo, fro[m] which Moses viewed the Holy Land (Deut. 34:1). The main claim to fame, however, is a mosaic map of [the] Holy Land, centered in Jerusalem. [It] is the oldest known map of the Ho[ly] Land, dating from the reign of the emperor Justinian (A.D. 560-565)[.] It is a good record of what was kn[own] about Jerusalem at that time.*

ABOVE: *The great triumphal arch, built in honor of the visit of the emperor Hadrian in A.D. 129, still stands.*

RIGHT: *This is the southern of the two main intersections of Roman streets in Jerash that had a tetrapylon, four massive piers connected by four arches.*

# *Jerash*&MEDEBA

The Roman road can still carry traffic.

# PETRA

At the end of the canyon you come upon the magnificent El Khazneh, "the treasury." It is a breathtaking sight. It was actually a tomb.

ABOVE: *About fifty miles south of the Dead Sea on the King's Highway is Petra the glory of Jordan. Petra was known as Sela in Scripture (II Kings 14:7; Isa. 16:1; 42:11). Both words mean "rock"(Judg. 1:36). It became the capital of the Nabatean kingdom of Arabia. The usual way of getting to the city is on horseback through the siq (the narrow canyon). The siq was a formidable defense in the ancient world. Pompey tried to take Petra in 63 B.C. and failed. A mere handful of men could hold off an army in that narrow canyon.*

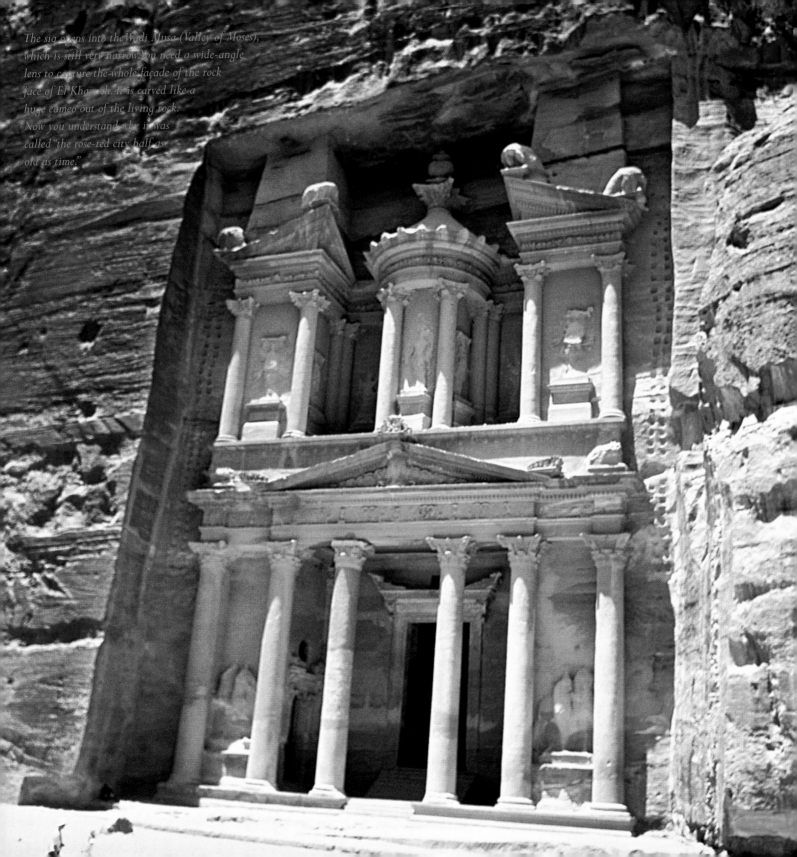

The siq opens into the Wadi Musa (Valley of Moses),
which is still very narrow. You need a wide-angle
lens to capture the whole façade of the rock
face of El Khazneh. It is carved like a
huge cameo out of the living rock.
Now you understand why it was
called "the rose-red city half as
old as time."

From the inside of El Khazneh you face the canyon wall. The shade is perceptibly cooler.

# PETRA

ABOVE: *Swirls of rose-red sandstone adorn every surface.*

ABOVE: *Everywhere you look there are caves. The bushes are oleander.*

LEFT: *The colors can range from white to brown, but rose red predominates.*

# PETRA

LEFT: *The Roman theater dates to the first century A.D. and could seat three thousand people. The holes in the back wall are caves that have been cut into during the original carving out of the theater.*

LEFT: *It is interesting to view the theater from the caves on the opposite side of the valley.*

RIGHT: *The time I visited Petra in the summer of 1978, as it happened, was the day after Queen Noor had married King Hussein. She came in by helicopter to bring her American family to see Petra. Members of the Desert Legion drove her and her family through Petra. She was in the first Land Rover, waving and smiling at everyone. I climbed up to the top of the cliff to get a good view of the valley just as her caravan drove through.*

# PETRA

LEFT: *Goats do find forage in very hot places.*

TOP: *There are places where a good part of the Roman paving is still in place.*

ABOVE: *Beyond the Holy Land there are many other lands mentioned in the Bible that are important in the biblical record. Joseph and Moses were certainly familiar with the river Nile (Gen. 41:45-46; Exod. 2:1-10). This scene of the Nile as it flows through present-day Cairo has a very different appearance from the way it looked in their day. But a supplemental work on lands of the Bible is another project.*

# WHERE CAN I FIND?

Many travelers wish to bring home some mementos of their travels. Almost anything can be found in the shops of Jerusalem or Tel Aviv or in hotel gift shops, generally for a king's ransom. But where are the best places to purchase souvenirs at a reasonable cost?

**Carved olive wood.** The olive wood factories are at Bethlehem. Since the carvings are done there, it is best to save your money and wait until you reach Bethlehem to purchase such things. There is a vast selection of any quality carving. Whether you are looking for a single camel or a whole nativity scene, Bethlehem is the place to find it.

**Hammered copper and brass.** Accho is one of the places where metal plates, bowls, trays, and other works are actually made.

**Enameled metal.** Nazareth has many shops that have good selections. The pieces are often designed specifically for Christians, Jews, or Muslims. The same piece will be available in many different decorations and colors.

**Glass, tiles, and pottery.** These pieces are fired in the Hebron area. Depending on the political circumstances,

you may not be able to get there, but if you can, there are good finds.

**Museum replicas.** The gift shop at the Israel Museum has many replicas of oil lamps, the Dead Sea Scrolls, and other things. There is a shop at the Shrine of the Book that has a different collection available. The Rockefeller Museum gift shop has yet a different selection. There is also a gift shop at the Hazor Museum.

**Genuine antiquities.** There are government-licensed antiquity dealers in Caesarea, right in the middle of the ruins, and in Samaria at the edge of the bus parking lot. They will give you a certificate of authenticity. Expect to pay a high price. There are also dealers in Jerusalem. Expect to pay a much higher price.

**Israeli postage stamps.** There are stamp shops in Jerusalem and Tel Aviv. They can also be purchased in the USA.

**Israeli coins and medals.** Israel Government Coins and Medals Corporation, Ltd. 5, Ahad Ha'am Street, Jerusalem. They also deal in mail orders.

# WHAT SHOULD I TAKE?

Keep passport, traveler's checks, and money exchange sheet within reach. (Have a separate list of the serial numbers of the checks packed.)

## Personal toiletries

Shower cap, 1 bar of soap, clogs for shower, shampoo.
Toothbrush, paste, floss, collapsible cup.
An extra washcloth and face towel.
Deodorant, suntan lotion, shaving lotion.
AC/DC kit for razor or small dryer (large ones blow fuses).
Moistened towelettes (individually wrapped, removed from box, put in Ziploc baggie).
1 roll of toilet paper (remove cardboard center and pack flat; the kind supplied may range from postage stamp size to sandpaper softness).

## Laundry needs

Clothesline and pins kit.
Inflatable hanger or a regular one.
Spot remover pads.
Laundry detergent mixed with dry bleach and water softener (put in baggies; when bags are empty, use to organize small souvenirs).
Sewing kit with safety pins and several colors of thread.

## Medication

Carry written prescriptions for all medications and eyeglasses.
Be sure medications are labeled.
Aspirin, medicine for upset stomach.
Sunglasses.

## Mailing needs

It is necessary to buy postage from the country you visit.

Preaddressed labels and envelopes for friends back home.

Buy postcards (your pictures may not all come out).

## Greatly desirable items

Your Bible.

Travel log book.

A point and shoot camera (with all the film you can afford).

Or a digital camera with laptop computer for storing flashcard photos.

If you want timed photos at night, bring a folding tripod.

Baggie snack pack for candy, nuts, breath mints, etc.

Travel alarm.

Note pad and pens.

## Luggage

One large, sturdy piece of luggage (to check through).

One small, folding piece you can pack in the large one (You tend to come back with more than you started with!)

One piece of hand luggage or camera bag you carry at all times.

## Clothes in general

Cotton and cotton blend for comfort.

Real hiking shoes (good arch support, well broken in); if you are used to sneakers, be sure you can walk in them hour after hour.

Dress shoes (dinner at 8).

Bathing suit (if you plan to swim in the Med, the Dead, the Red).

## Clothes for women

Skirts, blouses, jacket, 1 sweater, 1 good dress (dinner at 8).

Culottes or loose slacks (for climbing among ruins, riding camels, etc.).

Sun hat (inexpensive garden hat with tie).

Support hose if you are not used to walking.

Cotton socks.

One small scarf and one scarf large enough to cover your shoulders. (Without it, you will not be allowed in churches, synagogues, and mosques.)

## Clothes for men

4 or 5 shirts (or take 2 and wash one every day).

1 good pair of slacks and one sport coat (dinner at 8).

Two pairs of hiking slacks or jeans.

Belt.

Sweater for nighttime activities.

Sun hat or cap with visor (otherwise, one afternoon in the sun will take the skin off your nose for the whole trip).

Razor.

No shorts, or you will not be allowed in churches, synagogues, and mosques.

Remember, if you have small children at home, one small stone with the name of the place it was found written on it (Jerusalem) may be more valuable than gold. Stick them in baggies as well.

# ILLUSTRATED RESOURCES

## BOOKS

Alon, Azaria. *The Natural History of the Land of the Bible.* New York: Paul Hamlyn, 1969, 276 pp.

Amster, Joel, ed. *Israel in Three Dimensions.* Moshav Ben Ami, Israel: Original Creations, Ltd., 1998. [3-D photos with glasses]

*Art and History of Jerusalem: The Holy City–3000 Years.* Florence, Italy: Bonechi Publishing Group, 2000.

Barnavi, Eli. *A Historical Atlas of the Jewish People.* New York: Schocken Books, 1992, 299 pp.

Bruce, F. F. *In the Steps of Our Lord.* Grand Rapids: Kregel, 1993, 64 pp.

Bruce, F. F. *In the Steps of the Apostle Paul.* Grand Rapids: Kregel, 1995, 64 pp.

Bruce, F. F. *Jesus and Paul: Places They Knew.* Nashville: Thomas Nelson, 1981, 128 pp.

Bourbon, Fabio, and Enrico Lavagno. *The Holy Land.* Vercelli, Italy: White Star S.r.l., (Barnes & Noble) 2001, 228 pp.

Comay, Joan. *The Jerusalem I Love.* Tel Aviv, Israel: Leon Amiel Publisher, 1976, 158 pp.

Dehan, Emmanuel. *Our Visit to Israel.* Tel Aviv, Israel: By the Author, 1981, 224 pp.

Devir, Ori. *Off the Beaten Track in Israel: A Guide to Beautiful Places.* New York: Adama Books, 1989, 208 pp.

Dorling Kindersley Travel Guides. *Jerusalem and the Holy Land.* New York: Dorling Kindersley Publishing, Inc., 2000, 304 pp.

Dowley, Tim, and Heike Goshen. *Next Year in Jerusalem.* Eugene, Oreg.: Harvest House Publishers, 1995, 255 pp.

Foure, Catherine, ed. *The Holy Land.* Knopf Guides. New York: Alfred A. Knopf, Inc., 1995, 2000, 480 pp.

Gafni, Shlomo S. *The Glory of Jerusalem: An Explorer's Guide.* Jerusalem: The Jerusalem Publishing House, 1978, 128 pp.

Gafni, Shlomo S. *The Glory of the New Testament.* Jerusalem: The Jerusalem Publishing House, 1983, 256 pp.

Godfrey, Fr., O.F.M. *A Pilgrim in the Holy Land.* Herzlia, Israel: Palphot Ltd., n.d., 144 pp.

Hastings, Arthur F. *In His Honor: A Pictorial Journey Through the Early Years of the Christian Church.* Muskego, Wis.: H.H.P. Publishing, Inc., 1994, 288 pp.

Khoury, Waleed. *See the Holy Land.* Jerusalem: Asharq—Public Services, n.d., 144 pp.

Lesberg, Sandy. *The Walls of Jerusalem.* Indianapolis, Ind.: Bobbs-Merrill, 1976, 125 pp.

*Lion Photoguide to the Bible.* Tring, Herts, England: Lion Publishing, 1981, 1983, 287 pp.

Magi, Giovanna. *Jerusalem.* Firenze, Italy: Bonechi Publishing Group, 1990 (Steimatzky), 64 pp.

Magi, Giovanna. *Masterpieces of the Israel Museum.* Florence, Italy: Bonechi Publishing Group, 1985, 64 pp.

Magi, Giovanna. *The Holy Land.* Florence, Italy: Bonechi Publishing Group, 1992 (Steimatzky), 128 pp.

Neumann, Anton. *Israel.* New York: Gallery Books, 1985, 72 pp.

Palphot, Ltd. *Israel: Pictorial Guide & Souvenir.* Herzlia, Israel: Palphot, Ltd., n.d., 128 pp.

Palphot, Ltd. *Jerusalem: Pictorial Guide & Souvenir.* Herzlia, Israel: Palphot, Ltd., n.d., 72 pp.

Pax, Wolfgang E. *In the Footsteps of Jesus.* Tel Aviv, Israel: Leon Amiel Publisher, 1975, 224 pp.

Paz, Uzi. *Wild Flowers of the Holy Land.* Secaucus, N.J.: Chartwell Books, Inc., 1979, 100 pp.

Pearlman, Moshe. *In the Footsteps of the Prophets.* Tel Aviv, Israel: Leon Amiel Publisher, 1975, 223 pp.

Porter, J. R. *The Illustrated Guide to the Bible.* New York: Oxford University Press, 1995, 288 pp.

Porter, R. F., S. Christensen, and P. Schiermacker-Hansen. *Field Guide to the Birds of the Middle East.* London: T. & A.D. Poyser, 1996, 460 pp.

Sacks, Eliezer, ed. *2000 Years of Pilgrimage to the Holy Land.* Tel Aviv: Cordinata, Ltd., 1998, 168 pp.

Schiller, Ely, ed. *The Old City: The First Photographs of Jerusalem.* Jerusalem: Ariel Publishing House, 1978, 252 pp.

Tal, Duby, and Moni Haramati. *Golan Skyline*. Israel: Albatross Aerial Photography, Ltd., 1997, 208 pp. [All aerial photos]

Tal, Duby, and Moni Haramati. *Jerusalem Skyline*. Israel: Albatross Aerial Photography, Ltd., 1993, 2001, 238 pp. [All aerial photos]

## CD-ROM (WIN/MAC)

*A Walk in the Footsteps of Jesus*. Hiawatha, Iowa: Parsons Technology, Inc., 1997.

*Jerusalem: An Interactive Pilgrimage to the Holy City*. New York: Simon & Schuster, Interactive, 1995.

*Pathways Through Jerusalem*. Nanuet, N.Y.: Future Vision Multimedia Inc.

## VIDEOS

*Israel*. Bnei Brak, Israel: Steimatzky, Ltd.

*Jerusalem Potpourri*. Jerusalem, Israel: Shiba Ltd.

*Jerusalem: Within These Walls*. Washington, D.C.: National Geographic Society.

*Treasures of the Holy Land*. Jerusalem, Israel: The Israel Museum.

# SCRIPTURE INDEX

# MUSEUM INDEX

*Fee required

Acre Municipal Museum, Acre.
　　Roman glass, Ottoman relics.
Antiquities Museum of Tel Aviv-Yafo. *
　　10 Mifratz Schlomo Street, Jaffa.
　　Stone inscriptions, idols.
Arad Museum and Visitors Center, Arad.
　　28 Ben Yair Street, Arad.
　　Reconstructed temple.
Bar David Institute of Jewish Art.
　　Kibbutz Bar'am
　　Oil lamps, glass.
Beit Gordon, south of Sea of Galilee. *
　　Kibbutz Deganya Alef.
　　Natural history: mammals, birds, flowers, fossils, and minerals.
Beit Miriam Museum (By appointment: tel. 03-965958)
　　Kibbutz Palmahim, between Tel Aviv and Ashdod.
　　Statuettes, ossuary, tomb relics.
Beit Pinchas Biological Institute: Gan Ha'em Museums. *
　　124 Hatishbi Street, Mount Carmel, Haifa.
　　Botanical garden, zoo, nature museum.
Beit She'an Museum of Archaeology.
　　North of City Center.
　　Relics from the excavations of Beit She'an.
Beit She'arim Catacombs and Museum. *
　　Jezreel Valley.
　　Cave tombs, sarcophagi, inscriptions.
Beit Sturman. *
　　Kibbutz Ein Harod, Jezreel Valley.
　　Roman milestones, natural history.
Beit Ussishkin. *
　　Kibbutz Dan.
　　Archaeological finds from Dan, natural history.

Bible Lands Museum, Jerusalem
　　Corner of Granot and Burla streets
　　Artifacts illustrating the Bible.
The Burnt House. *
　　13 Tiferet Yisrael Street, Old City, Jerusalem.
　　An actual home destroyed in A.D. 70; pottery, stone weights.
Caesarea Museum: Beit Hanna Sennesh.
　　Kibbutz Sdot Yam.
　　Roman archaeological finds from Caesarea Maritima.
The Citadel Museum. *
　　Tower of David, Old City, Jerusalem.
　　An archaeological site and displays.
Coral World Underwater Observatory and Museum. *
　　Eilat.
　　Fish and coral from the Red Sea.
Dagon Museum.
　　Plumer Square, Haifa.
　　History of grain, ancient sickles, statues.
Ein Dor Museum of Archaeology. (By appointment: tel. 06-768111)
　　Kibbutz Ein Dor, near Mt. Tabor.
　　Stone tools, pottery, oil presses.
Eretz Israel Museum (Land of Israel Museum). *
　　2 University Street, Ramat Aviv, Tel Aviv. (30 acres).
　　Pavillions for copper mining, ceramics, thousands of coins, ancient glass, an actual excavation of Tel Qasile, etc.
Franciscan Biblical Museum.
　　Church of the Flagellation, Via Dolorosa, Old City, Jerusalem.
　　Artifacts, coins from different locations.
Golan Archaeological Museum. *
　　Katzrin.
　　Arrowheads, oil lamps, coins, structures of buildings.

Greek Orthodox Patriarchate Museum. *
   Christian Quarter, Old City, Jerusalem.
      Sarcophagi, Roman glass, fragments of churches.
Hazor Museum. *
   Kibbutz Ayelet Hashahar.
      Basalt lions, pottery, stone vessels, cylinder seals.
Reuben and Edith Hecht Museum.
   University of Haifa, Mount Carmel, Haifa.
      Figurines of animals, anthropoid coffins, seals, weights.
Hula Nature Reserve and Visitors Center. *
   Yesud Hama'ala.
      Fish ponds, birds, flowers, nature trail.
Israel Museum and Shrine of the Book. *
   Ruppin Boulevard, Jerusalem.
      The Dead Sea Scrolls, jars, historical display of
      archaeological findings, Jewish heritage, coins, art
      gallery, etc.
Lehmann Museum and Hammath Tiberias Synagogue. *
   Tiberias.
      Pottery, mosaic synagogue floor.
Makhtesh Ramon Visitors Center. *
   Mitzpe Ramon National Park, Negev.
      Desert crater, geology, desert animals, and plants.
Edward and Helen Mardigian Museum. *
   Armenian Quarter, Old City, Jerusalem.
      First-century frescoes, Armenian mosaics and tiles.
Museum of the Negev. *
   1 Ha'atzmaut Street, Be'er Sheba.
      Tools, copper vessels, 4-horned altar, oil lamps, glass.
Museum of Regional and Mediterranean Archaeology. *
   Kibbutz Nir David, Jezreel Valley.
      Artifacts from Beit She'an, mosaic synagogue floor,
      reconstructed temple, classical Greek vases.
Nahariya Municipal Museum.
   19 Gaaton Street, Nahariya.
      Canaanite artifacts, incense burners from a local
      temple, remains of a Phoenician vessel.
Nahsholim Museum. *
   Kibbutz Nahsholim, Hof Dor.
      Underwater archeology, stone anchors, finds from Tel Dor.

National Maritime Museum. *
   198 Allenby Road, Haifa.
      Models of Egyptian, Greek, Roman ships; stone
      anchors, amphorae found at sea.
Oppenheimer Diamond Museum. *
   1 Jabotinsky Street, Ramat Gan.
      Model of the high priest's breastplate with the 12 stones.
Revadim Archaeological Museum.
   Kibbutz Revadim.
      Finds from Tel Miqne (Ekron?); reconstructed oil
      press, jars, tools, 4-horned stone altar.
The Rockefeller Museum. *
   Suleiman Street, Jerusalem.
      Displays from every period and every part of the Holy
      Land: unique inscriptions from Megiddo, mosaic
      floors, gold jewelry, etc.
Shamir Regional Museum (By appointment: Tel.: 06-941941).
   Kibbutz Shamir.
      Dolmens, pillars, boundary markers, pottery.
Siebenberg House. *
   7 Hagitit Street, Jewish Quarter, Old City, Jerusalem.
      Guided tours through a unique house, filled with
      artifacts in stone, glass, bronze.
The Skirball Museum.
   Hebrew Union College, 13 King David Street, Jerusalem.
      Many artifacts from Tel Dan, Gezer, Aroer; a 4-horned
      altar; models of city gates.
The Wohl Archaeological Museum. *
   Hurvah Square, Jewish Quarter, Old City, Jerusalem.
      Herodian mansions underground beneath Yeshivat
      Hakotel, a religious school; beautiful mosaic floors,
      many artifacts in display cases.
Yad Vashem.
   Mount of Remembrance, Jerusalem.
      A deeply moving memorial to the victims of the
      Holocaust.
Yotvata Museum and Visitors Center. *
   Kibbutz Yotvata.
      Techniques of copper smelting; stone molds.

# INDEX OF PLACES